Cheese
In the Time of
Glasnost and Perestroika

By Tony Kutter

To Helen

Tony

Dear reader

 PERESTROIKA literally means restructuring of their political and economic system. GLASNOST means openness and transparency. This was a new concept for Soviet citizens to have freedom of expression. Communism was coming apart under its own weight. Mikhail Gorbachev was forced to make drastic changes which lead to the collapse of communism. It was a disastrous economic and political revolution which created dire consequence for ordinary Russians. In the west we view it as the end of the cold war. Mikhail Gorbachev become the most hated man in Russia for destroying the Soviet Union. Agriculture was in a sorry state of affairs. Food wasn't arriving on store shelves. Most of the free world did not comprehend the trauma.

Dedication

I'd like to dedicate this book to my family,
My wife Trudy and my four children Andrew, Martin, Kristina and Thomas who all urged me to write this book.

To three Washington-based agencies that funded my
31 trips to Russia in 12 years:
- Land O'Lakes International Development Cooperative
- CNFA : Citizens Network Foreign Affairs
- ACDI-VOCA: Agricultural Cooperative Development International and Volunteers in Overseas Co-operative Assistance

Russian Agriculture from Communism to Capitalism

Tony Kutter's 12 Years in the Former Soviet Union Developing the Cheese Industry

Prologue

Suffering in Russia has become a cultural cliché (1990 -1996)

The Russian people were facing agricultural crises, a devalued ruble, a cash-strapped government, horrible economy and rising anti-Semitism, when Galina Starovoitova, a liberal reform minded member of the Duma, was gunned down outside her home. Anna Polikovsakya and many other journalists and human rights activists were assassinated. It was always doubtful the killers would ever be brought to justice. Many Russians I have worked with are searching for a capitalistic solution to their economic ills. Many others are looking backward with nostalgia for the Soviet past and by repressing hope to cure their ills and bolster their hope and pride.

After 60 years of cheese manufacturing at Kutter's Cheese Factory in Pembroke, New York, I traveled to Russia 31 times as a volunteer, teaching cheese making in many plants in Russia. I set up a pilot cheese plant in St. Petersburg and culminated my efforts by constructing a cheese plant from the ground up in Siberia, shipping all the equipment from the U.S. I had the unique opportunity to travel freely into the hinterlands of the world's largest country.

Our news media was dominated by the tension caused by two completely different world ideologies during the Cold War. This was the general topic of most of our political discussions about current events. I recall vividly the end of the Second World War. Joseph Stalin declared the war was a consequence of capitalistic imperialism. He brought down upon Eastern Europe what Winston Churchill so eloquently phrased the Iron Curtain. The Cold War was inaugurated with all its chilling consequences as the Soviets spread their Marxist doctrine around the world and the US tried to prevent third world countries from being engulfed by communism.

Russia lost 20 million soldiers in World War II; millions more were exiled, imprisoned, or executed in the mass purges to follow. I never dreamed I would someday live with Russians in their homeland; learn to speak their language while attempting to help them make that transfer from a command economy to a free market democratic society.

By 1990 Russian agriculture had never been in such a sorry state of affairs since Dictator Stalin's massive collectivization of peasant farms in the Ukraine during the 1920s. Because of the lack of enthusiasm for collectivization by the Kulaks (tight fisted successful farmers), millions were exiled into Siberia only to perish. Millions died from the famine caused by the Soviet policy in an attempt of crushing Ukraine's nationalistic sentiments by grain confiscation.

In 1996 the Mennonite Central Committee in Akron Pennsylvania sent Ben Falk, a Mennonite fruit farmer from Ontario Canada, to ascertain the whereabouts of the Mennonite communities in Siberia. He returned seeking assistance in the form of a cheese plant to utilize milk from an 800 cow collective farm. The farmers had not been paid for their milk for over a year. They were desperate and wanted to know if I would oversee the building of a cheese factory. He said, "Every Mennonite in the world was praying I would accept this unique humanitarian challenge". I needed to assemble all equipment here in the United States, containerized it and ship it all to Europe to be transferred overland to Neudochino, a small settlement near Omsk in central Siberia where many oil refineries are located to refine oil from Northern Siberia. The cheese factory is up and running today. Has it been successful? To a degree, yes, and the plan now: is to buy and process milk from neighboring villages, increase efficiency, and enlarge our production and demonstrate a profit generating enterprise. It hasn't happened yet. Every new business needs to pay some kind of protection money to survive in Russia's gangster capitalistic society. In1993 Russians had one of the worst grain harvests in 40 years. In Neudochino the grain crops died in the 100° heat with only l-2 inches of rain. We had no grain for the cattle. We fed them straw stalks with grain kernels removed which reduces their milk production to pitiful few liters per day. We had no money to buy grain. When American sends aid in the form of grain, food supplies, medicine and clothing it goes to a Russian customs warehouse and we must pay duty fees and storage charges. There is no alternative we have no recourse. Unscrupulous individuals may also try to sell the aid on the 'free" market.

I had no illusions of an economic miracle as Russians pursued democratic market reforms. Russia could not enter the new millennium with the high expectations Americans had when communism collapsed. Their living standards remained far behind the rest of Europe and the free world even today. About 1996 the International Monetary Fund has loaned $22 billon which Russia so desperately needed just to pay wage arrears and keep the ruble afloat.

It would be wrong to assume they cannot make the transition from a command economy to a free market economy in a 20 year generation. I volunteered my efforts and expertise hoping to see Russia become a world-class competitor in today's global economy.

Introduction

Writing a book has never been a goal of mine nor do I consider myself a writer. My family, friends and colleagues urged me to write this book and record my daily activities in my 12 years in Russia.

There are various ways to spell Russian names in English. I cannot verify the correct spelling in all of the words in this book. I tried my best to convey my own thoughts as factual and accurate as possible. I have tried to reflect on many facets of my travels in the former Soviet Union. From my daily cheese making operations, the obstacles I encountered and all the stories my co-workers told me about Russian history, I felt I needed to write this book. Many cheese factories that I worked at teaching Russians modern cheese making technology may seem somewhat repetitive but every part of Russia I traveled in was a unique experience. I made every effort to be as factual as possible.

Acknowledgements

Galina Holley

If there is one person I feel heavily indebted to it is Galina Holley, a Russian lady from the city of Pyatigorst. She came to our cheese factory with a friend who worked at the cheese factory, she spoke Russian. I had been to Russia several times and was making a supreme effort to learn Russian. I spoke a few words of Russian to her. She asked me if I could speak Russian. I told her I know only a few words but I have a longing desire to master this language. Several weeks went by and she called me and wanted to know if I could come to her home and she would help me with my Russian. She had been an interpreter in our local town traffic courts. Occasionally a Russian was apprehended for a traffic violation that spoke no English. She would be call upon to interpret.

Galina said, "I could teach you Russian, it will help me refresh my Russian". Attorneys often use a higher level of vocabulary in litigation. She would find it somewhat difficult searching for the correct interpretation. She said, "It has been 20 years since I left Russia and I need to revitalize my Russian". Needless to say I jumped at the opportunity with enthusiasm and I went to her house every Thursday for the next six years. All the years of my work in Russia I was able to communicate with my fellow workers in Russian which gave me huge credibility in the work place The Washington based Aid for International Development (AID) made numerous request for assignments for me in the Russian cheese industry because I had a basic knowledge of the language. It allowed me to travel freely to very remote parts of Siberia without a translator.

It was 1978 when Brezhnev was Premier of the Soviet Union a few Jewish Russians were allowed to immigrate after years of Soviet denial. Galina just finished a two-year course at a Russian Institute in foreign travel service. As a child she was a young pioneer and was urged to join the Konsomal to be recognized as an honorable Russian patriarch. However she kept it a secret from many people for personal reasons. If you wanted to attend a prestigious Russian University or become successful one had to be in good standing with the Communist Party.

She had a brother who was making friends with some Jewish families for the sole purpose of arraigning a marriage so the family could apply for immigration with his Jewish wife. This marriage to a Jewish person was to be annulled and they would separate.

Applications were submitted to local authorities then forwarded to Moscow for a visa. They were shocked when application was returned requesting an interview. During interview they try desperately to talk Galina into remaining in Russia. "Why would you want to leave Russia"? If you leave Russia you will never be able to return to your home land. Galina was under severe pressure and faced incredible amounts of interrogation. However, her steadfastness prevailed in her decision to immigrate with her family.

They boarded a train in Belarus and travel to Vienna, Austria. She traveled with her mother and grandmother; who was 90 years old. Her brother and uncle and his bride followed separately. When they arrived in Vienna, Catholic Charities sponsored them and gave them a choice of going to the United States, Canada, Australia or New Zealand. The family chose the US. They were destined for Mobile, Alabama, however there was a national disaster, a tremendous hurricane with wide spread destruction. There was a change in itinerary to Buffalo, New York.
Catholic charities also paid for all living expenses and were provided them with an apartment in Buffalo. Galina and her mother found employment soon afterwards.

Galina told me how she will always remember Catholic charities playing such an important part in her life's transition to a new country.

There is a very interesting history about the Jewish people referred to as "refuseniks". Many Jews applied for immigration and waited for 20 years. Often the Soviets gave no reasonable explanation for the prolong denial to immigrate, during these years the "refuseniks" were persecuted. Many lost their jobs. Many highly trained physicians, mathematicians and engineers were fired from their jobs. They were allowed only menial jobs such as janitors and street cleaners. In Russia your only employer was the communist government. Many "refuseniks" were monetarily supported by relatives outside of Russia. In most cases money was confiscated by the authorities.

The rise of Gorbachev's (Glasnost), greater openness and freedom made it possible for "refuseniks" to eventually leave but they had lost a great portion of their productive years living in fear of arrest and constant surveillance.

It must have been a profound experience to have a tremendous load taken off your mind when Galina's family crossed the border into the free world. I will always remember how much Galina meant to me every time I went to her home and we spoke Russian to together.

A Visit with the Former President of World Bank

I never fully understood the implications of the billions of dollars the International Monetary Fund and the World Bank involvement providing loans to shore up the ruble. The former president of the World Bank granted me an opportunity to speak to him about my involvement in agriculture and cheese manufacturing in Russia. It was after Russia defaulted that many Russians lost their meager savings. Barber Conable retired and lived in Alexander, NY just a few miles from me. He invited me to his home. After he answered many of my questions and concerns he said, "Tony you have got to write a book. You have much to share with everybody. I don't anyone who has traveled so widely in Russia."

KUTTERS CHEESE

APPEARS IN RUSSIA

TABLE OF CONTENTS

Family History

My father, Leo, was born in 1893 in Bavaria, Germany, one of 21 children. His mother died of after childbirth due to lack of medical attention. Only 13 of them survived infancy. At the age of 12, he was farmed out to work in the mountainous Alps assisting a cheese maker. They would take the cows up into the mountains in the spring and stay with them until winter when they would return to their villages with their cows.

His duties were to herd cows, milk them and carry cheese on an A-frame strapped to his back down the mountains into markets of the local villages and communities. This was the beginning of his cheese making vocation.

Leo Kutter was drafted into the German army for two years. He served in the infantry but before he finished his conscription, World War I broke out. He served until 1918, fighting in the trenches in France. He was taken prisoner of war by the French. He escaped and suffered from severe frostbite by hiding out in the cold winter all to no avail. When he returned home he found out the armistice had been signed and the war was over.

Germany was in economic chaos with rampant inflation. His mentor told him "you're a young man, not married and your future is uncertain here, you should go to America".

His name is recorded on a ship's manifest at Ellis Island in 1923. He had $16 in his pocket and was sponsored by his sister, Anna Kutter of Buffalo, NY. Arrangements were made for him to live in a boarding house on Jefferson Avenue in Buffalo. Anna urged him to come to Western New York, one of the six largest manufacturing metropolitan cities in America at the time.

Buffalo, at the turn of the century was the gateway to the west and hosted the Pan-American Exposition. It was called the "city of light" because of the hydroelectric power generated by power plants at Niagara Falls. Buffalo had the largest flour milling operation in the world, and Bethlehem steel was prominent in the city utilizing iron ore from the Mesabi Range in north eastern Minnesota. It was a railroad hub, pioneering aviation and booming automobile factories chose to locate there.

Leo Kutter first considered Wisconsin or Ohio because they were already noted for cheese manufacturing. German immigrants had been arriving in Buffalo in significant numbers since the early days of the 20th century. Much of Buffalo's culture was derived from German immigrants.

The time was referred to as the "Roaring 20s"; skilled laborers were needed in every facet of industry. Leo Kutter, the cheese maker, worked for the Hasselbeck Cheese Company a subsidiary of Borden Foods Inc.

In 1924 he operated a cheese factory in Cowlesville, New York for Hasselbeck. But it was his dream to start his own business. In

1929 the stock market crash was followed by the Great Depression which lasted until the start of the Second World War. His dream was squelched again during the Second World War because much of the milk was dried and shipped overseas for the war effort. There was no milk available for cheese making

He was urged to work at Curtiss Wright Corp. where they manufactured warplanes. As a World War I German soldier and now his brother-in-law were fighting on the German side he felt he wanted no part of making war materials. Peace is an ugly war to war weapon producers.

I was 10 years old at the time of the Normandy invasion of Europe. My mother had younger brothers fighting in the German army. All letters and communications were censored and family communication was cut off for years. When the first letter arrived from Germany my mother opened it with apprehension. She broke down in tears. She lost two of her younger brothers during the war. I had never seen my mother cry. It left a profound impact on my memory. My father hugged me and tried to console me as I was in tears.

In 1943 we moved to the town of Pembroke. In 1947 Leo Kutter started Kutter's Cheese Factory at age 55. He died in 1962 and his sons Tony and Richard continued the operation. We were the first cheese producers to integrate a satellite winery into our retail operation in 1990. We saw it as an opportunity to cross merchandise two great New York State agricultural products: wine and cheese.

Photo:
Leo Kutter and Flora Kutter, sons Tony and Richard. Dad was the cheesemeister, mom was his assistant and bookkeeper. Richard and Tony were delegated to work after school in the cheese factory and feed the hogs.
Dad had a hog farm adjacent to the cheese factory with 100 hogs. This consumed the whey generated from cheese making, augmenting our earnings in those early days.

We never had a marketing division or salesman to promote our cheese products. Distributors would approach us and inquire about handling our products. One of our biggest distributors was Heluva Good Cheese Company in Sodus, New York. Dietz and Watson of Philadelphia are now owners of the corporation.

I am a director for the New York State Cheese Makers Association. At one of our meetings a representative from Aid for International Development (AID) in Washington DC approached me and said they were looking for cheese manufacturers to volunteer to work in the former Soviet Union. I filled out a resume, sent it to Washington and I was asked to participate. This project assignment culminated in building a cheese plant in St. Petersburg. It also set up the opportunity to travel 3000 miles from Moscow into the heart of Siberia to a village called Neudochino and build a cheese factory from the ground up with all U.S. equipment. I ended up making 31 trips to Eurasia over a period of 12 years. I traveled all over the former Soviet Union working and teaching at different cheese plants and Universities.

Washington Based Agencies
Funded by Aid for International Development
ACDI/VOCA

Agricultural Cooperative Development International and Volunteers in Overseas Cooperative Assistance is a U.S. based private nonprofit development organization that advances our objectives in new emerging democracies and developing countries. Their mission is to identify and open economic opportunities for farmers and other related enterprises by promoting democratic principles and sound management concepts. ACDI/VOCA provides a mix of volunteers and consultants to travel to countries helping new entrepreneurs establish private farms and agribusinesses.

Citizens Network for Foreign Affairs (CNFA)

A major public private sector was created in Washington DC by the Citizens Network in 1991 to respond to the historic events taking place in the former Soviet Union. The basic objectives of the volunteer program were to stimulate agribusiness development, to further agricultural privatization and to strengthen both the private farmer and food processing enterprises in Russia.

Cheese Plant in St. Petersburg
October 15, 1994

Jack Quatermous was an equipment representative from Rochester, NY. He called on us in Corfu, NY on a regular basis to supply our cheese factory with equipment. He approached me to ask if I could assist putting together a cheese operation in St Petersburg, Russia. He had assembled a team including an attorney, Jim Shue and a Russian businessman, Victor Bezilevich from St Petersburg. I could not make a decision at that time because I had committed myself to travel to Korea.

I was drafted and served in the US army during the Korean War. By 1994 my wife and I with our friends Barbara and Bob Brady,

3

a fellow veteran, had an opportunity to revisit the country of Korea at the invitation of their government. They were honoring all Korean War veterans for the sacrifices they made that made Korea a democratic society and one of the most viable Asian economies.

In 1995 I committed myself to my most rewarding but challenging projects yet, culminating in 31 trips all across the Soviet Union. Projects and assignments included putting together cheese plants, training Russians in new product development and conducting teaching seminars at agricultural universities.

Russia in the early 1990s was a country where food was unavailable on grocery store shelves. Soviet citizens were standing in lines for hours to obtain basic food supplies.

The Soviet collapse had begun already in 1985. After 40 years of Soviet military buildup at the expense of domestic development, economic growth was at a standstill. War in Afghanistan and a dramatic drop in oil prices bankrupted the country. Many recent historians say President Ronald Reagan made a bold move when he increased our military preparedness by pushing through increases in our military budget. The Soviet Union just couldn't compete. Like a giant poker game, the US kept raising the ante; Russia finally folded. In 1990 when the World Wide Web was created, citizens obtained instantaneous and easy access to information from all parts of the globe. This led to greater political and social demands for freedoms. An international whirlwind of rhetoric criticizing Mikhail Gorbachev was unleashed which led to Glasnost (reform) and Perestroika (openness). Inflation skyrocketed and left a majority of Russian people in poverty. Agriculture was in a sorry state of affairs.

Shipping a Pilot Cheese Plant to St. Petersburg

A consortium called International Food And Beverage Co. represented by Americans and Russians requested I send a resume to Citizens Network for Foreign Affairs in Washington, They accepted my application to volunteer. They provided me with a visa, all other essential documents and funded all my travel expenses. I proceeded to put together the equipment to manufacture American style cheese in an existing dairy in St Petersburg.

I assembled all the equipment I needed to make small, experimental batches of cheese. We containerized the factory for shipment to St Petersburg Russia. It left from Geneva NY in March of 1995.

Three weeks later on April 18, 1995 I was packing a suit case, determining if everything was in order, and not knowing what to expect. I couldn't have done it without assistance and support of my wife Trudy.

My plane was delayed out of Buffalo, but still arrived at Kennedy International with ample time to make the connecting flight to Helsinki, Finland. I boarded the plane to Helsinki, watched a movie and tried to sleep. Arriving in Finland, we disembarked from the plane for a three hour layover. It was 37 F degrees, drizzly and dreary. The airport was empty.

April 19, 1995

In Helsinki the airport was outside of the city surrounded by rain soaked pine forests. This was the Finnish Lapland where reindeer live, very flat landscape.

We boarded KLM airlines for St Petersburg, with many Russians aboard. They were all packed in the smoking section to the rear of the plane. The small section reserved for non-smokers was almost empty.

My first glimpse of St. Petersburg, Russia from the air was overwhelming and shocking. There were many huge gray apartment houses. It was a warm spring day in St. Petersburg when I arrived late in the evening. Much to my surprise, it didn't get dark until 10 PM. My first impression was how gray, dull and dreary the airport was. Airports in the US are usually of more modernistic design.

Jack Quatermous from the International Food and Beverage Inc., (the joint Russian American venture) was there to greet me. We hailed a taxi cab. I was surprised at the poor conditions of Russian taxi cabs, but they were inexpensive. When hailing a cab any automobile driver may stop and you can negotiate the fare before you enter.

When entering the city I was astounded. It looked just like the pictures of Eastern Europe in the old National geographic magazines I read when I was a child.

We went out to dinner and then walked around the city.

J.S.C. Petrolact

Vasilenko Gennady Karpovich, Director
Litvinova Irena Iosifovna, Deputy Director

This dairy operation was presently operating in a former church having significant historical architectural features. The preservation and historical Society of St. Petersburg has designated this building to return to its original status as a Christian church of the Fedorov's Icon of the Virgin.

The government of St. Petersburg has provided J.S.C. Petrolact with a land lot to establish a modern dairy and cheese production, curing and packaging plant based on participation of foreign partners and investors. The International Food and Beverage Co. has been asked if we could provide equipment and packaging machinery.

About 25,000 tons of hard cheese is consumed per year in St. Petersburg. All of it is delivered from different regions of Russia and from abroad as there is no natural cheese production in the city.

Jim Shue and I made a complete study and advised them on different lines of dairy equipment available in the United States.

There is a possibility that we could have the director, Gennady Karpovich come to the US to observe different cheese facilities.

I wanted to take some small packaging equipment to St. Petersburg to demonstrate new techniques in packaging design, possibly expanding their own cheese making operation. This would depend on whether they received financing and we have to resolve our own problems with some of their delinquent debt. We need to overcome all their deficiencies in our effort to promote market reform and privatization.

My very first day of my assignment is when all my problems began. My equipment wasn't cleared through customs. This gave me an opportunity to tour the city of St. Petersburg, a great place to study the history of Russia and absorb its ancient culture. Russia's history is very dramatic and reads like a novel. I never expected it would be days before I could make cheese. Here is a brief synopsis of my observations.

April 20, 1995

I met my translator, Tatiana Churina. She was very proficient and was eager to meet me. We went to dairy #2 where they processed milk and made Russian cheese. It was a beautiful building, previously a church. We took a tour of the facility. I never have seen a place in need of so many repairs. At this dairy facility I met Maria. (I wish I could remember her last name). She was in charge of cheese making. Later that day we all went to a trade show at the convention hall in St. Petersburg. The fledging company had a booth at the show. We left the food show and took a taxi to our hotel, Octayaberskya, named in honor of the October 1917 Bolshevik Revolution. On the way we drove by the Hermitage; Russia's largest art museum. In front of the building I saw the square where the Bolshevik revolution started. I freshened up in my hotel and went to a restaurant for a delicious meal. I had my first bowl of borscht and it was quite tasty. We all had much to talk about anticipating our next move while contemplating making our first American-style cheese.

April 21, 1995

Jack Quatermous picked me up at the hotel. We went to the dairy and with Irena Litvinova, Tatiana and Maria and discussed at length the process of cheddar cheese curd production. I carried with me cheeses of various flavors. We all discussed the assessment and procurement of milk and its quality. I tested some Russian milk and determined its quality poor, not suitable for making cheese. We discussed buying milk from Finland because the Finns would assure us of low bacteria counts and quality milk. This alternative was too expensive so we decided to look for a Russian farm who could assure us their milk would be of good quality if we were willing to pay a premium price. I was quite surprised when Maria said, "Tony, I don't believe you will be happy with results from the quality of milk

6

we have". I realized her opinion was invaluable to this cheese factory, I agree with her understanding of bacteriology and what constitutes good quality milk

Our equipment arrived at customs. We discussed installing vats and equipment and hooking up steam. I felt we had a very productive meeting. They gave me an office with a desk. That evening we went to a restaurant, had dinner and we spoke about our business and our joint venture. We sat in the restaurant till midnight toasting each other with vodka.

Jack and Maria

April 22, 1995

Today is a day off for me. I attempted to study my Russian this morning but I am still suffering from jet lag and vodka. The most difficult part of my early years in Russia was learning the language. It certainly gives one a great deal of credibility when they can converse with fellow workers without an interpreter.

I just can't believe how warm it is, sunny and 60°F. We think Russia is always cold. All of Russia lies north of the state of Maine and it stretches across nine time zones. St. Petersburg is an intriguing and beautiful city. When it comes to restaurants it is most cosmopolitan. There are many foreign restaurants here and we decided to go to a German managed restaurant. We enjoyed bratwurst, sauerkraut and a good Warsteiner German beer.

The next day we hailed a taxi and went to the Hermitage, which means the secluded retreat, or residence of a hermit. This is the largest and oldest art museum in the world. It was founded in 1764 by Catherine the Great and open to the public since 1852. Only a small part of this collection is on permanent display, since it comprises nearly 3,000,000 items including the largest collection of paintings in the world. If you would study each item for two minutes, day and night, with no days off it would take several years to see entire collection.

The collection occupies a large complex of six buildings, including the Winter Palace and former residence of the Russian Czars. Of those six buildings only the small Hermitage and old Hermitage are open to the public. The grandeur is incomprehensible.

Many years ago I purchased a Russian sculpture called "Farewell Kiss by Lancery. Its subject is a Russian Cossack who was riding off to war to defend the borders. He is reaching down to grab his wife to kiss her good-bye before he sped off on his horse. It was cast in a Russian foundry in 1870. Jack Quatermous was very impressed and said he would never meet another person who had an art object by an artist whose work was displayed in the Hermitage .After four hours we had to leave because our minds couldn't absorb any more culture. We went out for dinner and then to a flea market catering mostly to foreigners who are looking for Russian souvenirs. A young man approached me and really wanted to buy my jacket because of the LL Bean logo on it. I couldn't resist trading it for a set of Russian Matroska nesting dolls. He beamed with pleasure and immediately wore it to impress his friends.

Sunday, April 23, 1995

We went to the Russian Orthodox Church for Easter service. Easter service begins at midnight and continues to noon. As there are no pews to sit in, everyone must stand. I was amazed at how many elderly ladies had been standing since midnight. There were very few young people at the service.

A rebirth is underway in the Russian Orthodox Church. Under Stalin almost all churches were closed and some destroyed. If you attempted to practice religion it was frowned upon. You could never hold an important position or attain status in the Communist party. Currently opinion polls rate the Russian Orthodox Church as the institution they most respected. Only about 10% of Russians attend church regularly, mostly women. I was always quite astounded when people would ask me "do you really believe in God"? No one had ever had ever asked me that question. I always felt that too much focus on one religion causes one to not respect other people's beliefs and religion.

I found the Russian Orthodox Church to be very inspiring with all the icons and paintings throughout the churches. The typical onion shaped dome made its appearance in the mid-12th century with Christianization of Russia. The Russian church became a subject of Constantinople's art, icons and architecture. Traveling throughout Russia I encountered many small villages with churches that had deteriorated beyond repair. Many people were putting their meager savings and hard work into restoring these once magnificent structures.

On many of my flights there were missionaries. They were trying to convert the Russian Orthodox faithful to other religious faiths and often had plenty of financial backing to establish churches. This influx caused resentment among Russian people. I found it ironic that Boris Yeltsin, a former communist, who may or may not believe in God, sure believes in the power of the Russian Orthodox Church. Campaigning before the June 16 election, the Russian president seldom missed a chance to visit local churches, light candles before TV cameras or appear in public with patriarch Alexi II. Under Yeltsin, the white bearded patriarch secured a suite of offices in the Kremlin, a perk the church has not enjoyed since Czarist times.

Not to be outdone, Communist candidate Gennady Zyuganov also had to try to favor the church and its followers, visiting monasteries, scrapping atheism from his party platform and proclaiming at campaign rallies that Jesus was the first true bona fide communist.

Historic St. Petersburg

Smolny Cathedral was once used as an educational Institute for noble ladies. It was originally intended to be a central monastery, built to house Elizabeth, the daughter of Peter the Great after she was not allowed to take the throne and opted instead to become a nun. As soon as her predecessor was overthrown by a royal guard during a coup, Elizabeth decided to forget the whole idea of a stern monastic life and happily accepted the offer of the Russian throne.

Smolny is undoubtedly one of the masterpieces of the architect, Rastrelli, who also created the Winter Palace. Today the Cathedral is used primarily as a concert hall and the surrounding convent houses are offices and government institutions. During the revolution it was taken over by revolutionary forces to house their government.

Peter and Paul Fortress is also in St Petersburg. Inside the fortress is a Cathedral where lies the white marble tombs of most of the Romanov families. The remains of Peter the Great lie in the far right-hand corner. This is where the Romanov's first prisoner, Peter the Great's son Alexi, was beaten to death. It was Alexi, who was involved in a coup and plot against his father.

We had lunch and went on to visit St. Isaac's Cathedral. It was originally the largest cathedral in Russia, built between 1813 and 1858 to be one of most impressive landmarks of the Russian Imperial capital. 180 years later the gilded domes of St. Isaac's still dominate the skyline of St. Petersburg.

St Isaac's facades are decorated with sculptures and massive granite columns made of single pieces of red granite. The interior is adorned with incredibly detailed massive icons. Some of the columns are made out of malachite and lapis lazuli. A large, brightly colored stained glass window of the resurrection of Christ dominates parishioner's attention. This cathedral was designed to accommodate 14,000 standing worshipers. Closed in the early 1930s it has reopened as a museum. Today, church services are held at St Isaac's only on major occasions.

Following a long day absorbing Russian history and culture in St. Petersburg we stopped at a nice restaurant and dined on good Russian cuisine and a little more vodka. That evening I was very tired and went back to my hotel and had a good night's rest.

Monday, April 24, 1995

I went to the dairy plant where I met Marie and Tatyana to discuss cheese making factory procedures. We needed specific plans to setup equipment in an area that was selected for us. The equipment had arrived at customs. Of course there was a problem but I left the officials to work out the details. This was a joint venture between four Americans and several Russians. Victor Bezelivich, Jim Shue and Deputy Director Galina Meeheva were meeting to discuss the procurement of the equipment from customs. They were supposed to meet us at noon... they arrived at 4 PM.

I used the wait time to have my interpreter, Tatiana, teach me some basic Russian. This was a period in Russia when everything was so difficult for the average Russian due skyrocketing inflation. She was upset by the fighting against separatists in Chechnya because everybody had to serve two years in the Army and the war seemed so senseless. She said that we are bogged down in this war like you Americans were in Vietnam, with no end in sight and many casualties.

Our factory team finally arrived at 4:30 PM and told us they would continue their meeting in the morning. That seems the way they do things around here. That evening we had a party with all the people from our office staff to celebrate Jack's birthday. Everyone made a toast to the success of this joint venture.

April 25, 1995

Preparing Room for Cheese Equipment

I proceeded to go to the dairy to see the progress preparing the room for our equipment. Maria was there assisting some other people cleaning up the area and doing some painting. Jack asked me if I would prepare a duty statement for Maria. This is important in Russia, it's called protocol. I still hadn't heard anything about the equipment or how they were going to resolve the customs issue. I was becoming perturbed because I was unable to contact the Russian partners. They were usually in some meeting where I was not included. That afternoon I walked around the city to take some photographs and just observe life in the city. It was a windy day, dirt and pollution were severe. I felt I needed a shower when I got back to my room.

April 26, 1995

When I reported to the dairy this morning Maria and Andrei said they were still anxiously awaiting word about the equipment. It had been sitting at custom in St. Petersburg for the last three weeks. My contacts told me they needed $21,000 at customs, but were trying to negotiate the price to $1400. They had originally agreed at $1200. This is unreal, but I had convinced myself that this is not my problem. I told Tatyana to go home after she spent an hour on my Russian lessons.

There must be 200 people working in this dairy. I don't think they took in anywhere near the amount of milk we do in my plant in the US with 50 people. Maria said some days they couldn't get milk because many farmers haven't been paid and can't afford to feed the livestock. So they are slaughtering their cattle for meat.

That afternoon I had an opportunity to speak to a regional Russian agricultural Minister. He said that there was a steep decline in the number of dairy cows in Russia. This was having a severe effect on the country's dairy industry which was being forced to import increasing amounts of dairy products. Just in six months of 1995 the number of milk cattle in Russia declined by 6%, almost 670,000 head. The overall amount of milk for processing had declined by 57,000 tons. This has led to a fall in output of dairy products. Imports have obviously been the main beneficiary of the decline in Russian cattle herds. Russia imports 35% of its cheese and imports are growing rapidly. I can remember that during the cold war the Soviet Union said they had to import grain from Canada, US and Australia because of bad weather conditions and poor harvests. I was beginning to understand why the communist system put Russian agriculture in such a sorry state of affairs. I felt that if we could overcome all these problems in the agriculture industry, especially farming and milk processing, it would help recapture some of these markets.

During the Stalin era all of agriculture was organized into collective farms. All the cattle and all the belongings of the peasants were confiscated for the common good. These farms were totally subsidized. After the collapse of communism, most of these farms went bankrupt. I visited many farms and listened to farm director's nostalgia for former days. There were 400 people working on a farm I visited. I asked "Where are all these people?" They told me that many of the workers were retired but were still on the payroll.

When a collective farm went bankrupt, everyone took a cow home to keep on their small plot of land. They milked these cows and produced a cheese called tvorog. This they sold on the street or on the open market.

Russian women selling milk from their individual cows and farmers cheese made in their homes. Often they were selling some of their meager possessions trying to make a few rubles to put food on the table. These were such difficult times for ordinary Russian families. Whenever I was invited into a Russian home for a meal there was always lots of food on the table. They often told me that nobody in Russia is going hungry.

11

April 27, 1995

This morning I met John and Lou Tarr, a couple from Geneva, NY. They had a family farm and dairy plant serving the Geneva area. John retired and closed down the dairy operation. He was an excellent engineer who possessed great skill in servicing and operating automated milk packaging equipment.

Later I met John Tarr, Peter Shue and Victor Bozilovich, and the Russian general director of a dairy in Yekaterinburg Russia, Fillip Felosian. We discussed setting up milk packaging equipment. John Tarr was also a volunteer for Citizens Network for Foreign Affairs. He helped the company purchase used filling equipment to package milk and juices in paper containers. The Russian agricultural Ministry had passed laws mandating all milk would have to be packaged and not sold on the street out of tanker trucks. John Tarr rebuilt these milk packaging machines and shipped them to Russia. He came to Russia several times to set up these machines and trained Russians how to operate them. International Food and Beverage Corp. expanded its joint ventures with dairies in Yekaterinburg, Omsk, and Novosibirsk in Siberia.

On one occasion I had the opportunity to travel to Novosibirsk with John and Lou Tarr. This was my first trip to Siberia. John had to help them service a machine and they also wanted help to make some cheese. I carried cultures and some rennet with me. They said they would have a vat of milk ready. The next morning after we arrived we all went to the plant. John began working on his machine and I proceeded to make some cheddar cheese curd. The cheese that I made was unacceptable because of the poor quality of milk. I did some investigation and found the milk that I used was outdated milk returned from retail stores. They had pasteurized the milk at very high temperatures which denatures the proteins to increase shelf life. It had a three day shelf life and many of the stores did not have the proper refrigeration. No one can make quality cheese from poor raw material.

We disposed of this product and proceeded with some fresh milk. We were successful in producing a quality cheese. Everyone had an opportunity to witness our procedures for making cheese. They were not ready to produce cheese commercially because of some financial problems that I was not told about.

That evening we flew back to St. Petersburg hoping to find my equipment so I could begin making cheese. We were surprised that Andre and Maria had set up Russian equipment and were ready to make cheese.

Tomorrow is May first (May Day) a celebration of the social and economic achievements of the international labor movement. It is commonly celebrated in socialistic and communistic countries of the world, but only rarely in the United States or Canada. This holiday can actually be traced back to Chicago in 1890 during the labor protests. Sometimes referred to as the Haymaker Affair, it is generally considered to have been an important influence on the origin of the international observances for workers. The causes of the Haymaker incident are still controversial, although deeply polarized attitudes separated business and working-class people in the late 19th century. Chicago police action generally acknowledged as having precipitated the protest and its tragic aftermath.

When I arrived at the plant the next morning I learned May Day was a holiday for everybody. Many people arrived in my hotel to have dinner and enjoy the day off. Some of my Russian colleagues brought a bottle of champagne and invited Jack Quatermous and me to join them for dinner. I looked out the window above the city square. There was a large parade marching down the street with bands all carrying communist flags and banners edifying Lenin. They were handing out leaflets urging the restoration of communist control. I ran down to the street to take pictures. The Communist Party and their leader, Gennady Zyuganov, marched the three mile stretch to the Hermitage. I always remember during the Cold War seeing news of Russians parades in Moscow's Red Square. They displayed their military hardware and all the members of the politburo watched from the Kremlin wall. My Russian friends urged me to join

in the parade which I did. My American friends were astounded and said. "The CIA will have a thick file on you". I said "that's okay; at my age I am not planning a government career or needing clearance from the CIA".

The next morning after our celebration I arrived at the plant. We had milk and the Russian equipment was cleaned and sterilized and we were ready to start making some cheese. I was glad that I had carried my cultures, rennet and other ingredients in my suitcase. We made cheddar cheese curds and flavored them with garlic, dill and hot peppers. The following day we packaged this cheese into 6 ounces packages. Again, we received milk and made some cheddar cheese, this turned out to be excellent.

While Maria and I were making cheese, Tatyana came to me with some very good news. Much to my amazement, the container of equipment arrived and they wanted to know where to deliver it. We were on the second-floor of our building so we hired a crane which showed up very shortly afterwards. It lifted all the equipment out of the container and put it through a large opening in the side of the building and into the cheese room. Everything got even better because the cheese curd turned out to be excellent, as good as anything we could make in America. The following day we set up our

American equipment. My time was running out so I was very pleased that we could accomplish what we did after waiting so long for our equipment.

That evening we were all feeling elated and in good spirits about the success of our cheese operation. We all went out to dinner, bought some Georgian wine, Stalin's favorite, and brought some of our cheese curd. Everyone made a toast, drank some wine and tried the different flavored cheese curd.

After eating our dinner I asked one final question, how was the financial issue at customs resolved? We were informed by Jim Shue that he told them Tony was so disgusted and discouraged that he would never come to Russia again. Also, that he had Russian equipment and he was not going to pay $21,000. Customs will be stuck with this equipment and I didn't care what they did with it. We think they agreed on a price that was not revealed to me. I asked about the price and they said it wasn't for me to ask. Jim said "you beat the Russians at their own game". They gave me a bottle of the best Russian vodka to take home. My wife had made some small quilts that I presented to Tatyana and Maria. It was a personal gift and they were pleased.

We started packaging cheese curds and also decided to package snack foods on our packaging machinery such as mixed nuts and dried fruit. This was something new in Russia, carrying a package of snacks and some drinks. Even Coca Cola inquired about our operation but it was quickly determined that we were not in a position to take on the volume they needed.

That evening a friend of Jack's, Galena, who worked for Chevron, came from Moscow on the overnight train to meet us. I had moved my belongings out of my room and moved into Jack's apartment and let Galina use my room. I think she came to celebrate May Day in St. Petersburg.

May 2, 1995

Today was another holiday so we decided to take a trip to Vyborg. Jack bought train tickets for Galina, Tatyana and me. Vyborg is a seaport near the Finnish border on the Gulf of Finland where my equipment was unloaded. It was a beautiful city with influence of Finnish architecture. On the three-hour train ride and we rode fourth class. The train was in disrepair and quite dirty. Because Galina and Tatyana were interpreters we had a great time and some great conversations with young Russian college students who were anxious to speak to Americans. This gave me an opportunity to practice my Russian. Whenever I had spare time I engaged my interpreter to give a Russian lesson. We spent the whole day in Vyborg and had dinner at an old castle built in 1645. Peter the Great had his fortress there during his reigning years.

May 3, 1995

I went to the dairy and supervised another day of cheese making.

In the afternoon I had a long meeting with our accountant. I had to calculate the costs of the current production in rubles so we could figure the economics of future production. Tatyana was certainly excellent in interpreting our conversation, explaining economics when conducting business meetings. These are some of the problems we discussed.

    No 1- Farmers who hadn't been paid for milk

    No 2- Excessive manpower, they seem unable to come to grips with laying off people.

    No 3- Delinquent accounts receivable

    No 4- Maintaining cash flow, they feel the salaries come first.

May 4, 1995

I was invited to speak to the director of another processing plant. This plant was huge. It took up a city block. I was always astounded by the size of buildings built under communism. They made the typical Russian cheese called tvorog which was very good. They had a joint venture with Polish and German firms to make casein. They ran the factory one day and had a management disagreement which they could not resolve. There sat $1 million worth of new equipment and no way to resolve the situation for over a year. It had been very difficult for foreign investors involved in joint ventures dealing with Russians. That afternoon we went to a large dairy farm. They had 900 cows on this farm which is also part of a joint venture. The farm was well maintained and in good condition. We discussed herd yields in America. They were well aware that in order to be profitable, cows have to be bred to increase yields to compete with European dairy farmers.

That evening we all went out to dinner to a restaurant that was frequented by members of the Russian mafia. They wanted us to go into another part of the restaurant, exclusively for foreigners, but the prices were much higher. Jack, who could be very obstinate, said "I work with Russians so I can eat with Russians". After he said that the service really deteriorated.

May 5, 1995

I arrived at the cheese plant and Maria had the packing equipment set up to package cheese curd in 200g bags. We also made some onion flavored curd and that was a real hit. This cheese was labeled and again was distributed to employees in retail outlets for evaluation. We had only good complements everyone said they would buy it if they could afford it. I was kind of surprised when one lady said she liked the cheese but she wouldn't buy it "I would rather save my money and buy a beautiful dress because people can see what I am wearing not what I ate". I always noticed in the streets of St. Petersburg at how beautifully the ladies were dressed.

In the afternoon we had a meeting with the Chief Executive Officer. The meeting began with cognac and everybody had to give a toast. The CEO gave a long toast about the war in Leningrad and praised the current peace and friendship and understanding insuring our venture would succeed. We had a two-hour meeting where they unveiled blueprints for a grand new facility in St. Petersburg. The present facility in the church is going to be restored with use as a church or a museum once again.

Some of the problems we discussed at our meeting:
- Milk supply and quality
- Costs of production
- The solvency of the company
- Distribution
- Lack of buying power of an average Russian

Today is our last day here so, I spent the rest of the day with Tatyana and Maria going over the cheese making procedures and reviewing everything before I left. It was very emotional for everyone when we said goodbye.

That night Tatyana took Jack and me to a Russian ballet at the Mariinski Theater, one of the top Russian male dancers was on stage. I have never seen such a beautiful opera house and the performance was breathtaking. The costumes and stage settings were something to behold. There were no tickets available at the box office but she got some inexpensive tickets from scalpers in front of the theater. It was a beautiful way to end three weeks in Russia.

May 6, 1995

It was Saturday; I had a day off before I had to catch a plane back to the US. I decided that there was one very historic memorial I wanted to visit. It was the Piskariovskoye Cemetery. It was very sobering to me to witness so many pit graves with only a marker giving the date. One grave would have a marker August 10, 1942 the next pit grave August 17, 1942. Each individual grave contained hundreds of victims. For over 900 days St. Petersburg was under siege by the Nazis.

They cut off all water supplies, food, and fuel. Most of the victims died of starvation or froze to death. January 1943 the siege was broken and several hundred thousand people were evacuated from the city across frozen Lake Ladoga. The only route that connected the besieged city was over the main land. It is estimated that 800,000 people were buried in these mass graves in different cemeteries.

The Nazi siege was certainly the most tragic period in the history of the city, so much suffering and heroism. To older generations it brings up memories they will never forget. Touring the cemetery certainly was an emotional experience for me. I think it kind of numbed my mind that these events took place in my lifetime.

I returned to the apartment, packed my bags, made some lunch with Jack and drank a few shots of vodka. The next morning I got up at 5 am for a flight to the US.

Piskariovskoye Cemetery

Visiting this memorial can be a haunting experience an eternal flame burns constantly to memorialize the hundreds of thousands of victims who died of starvation and sickness during the 900 day siege. This picture shows only one small section, it goes on forever. There are 186 mass pit graves.

Only a stone block marks the date on the pit graves. The raised stone bocks have dates that are merely a week apart. How can war be so brutal?

May 7, 1995

I had a meeting at Citizens Network at 9:30 AM in Washington. I presented my final reports and then had a debriefing session. After that we went to Capitol Hill to the office of Bill Paxton, my congressman. After hearing about my experiences he was surprised that I was able to ship a pilot cheese plant to St. Petersburg, set it up and train Russians to make cheese and did it on such a small budget. I took a cab to the airport and caught a plane home. My wife and children were waiting for me when I arrived in Buffalo.

The following pictures are of the old monastery that we used as a cheese factory in St Petersburg. It is a national landmark.

My Second Trip to St. Petersburg

September 1, 1995

I received a call from Jim Shue asking me if I could return to St. Petersburg to continue work at the cheese plant. I contacted Citizens Network for Foreign Affairs and they quickly approved my trip and funding. I arrived in St Petersburg at 11:30 AM and Victor picked me up and took me to my hotel. At 3 PM I went to the cheese factory and met Maria and Andrei. They were trying to fix a paper filling machine that had broken down. After a brief meeting I left to go back to my hotel and made some lunch.

September 2, 1995

I went to the cheese plant where Maria was making cheese. I

worked with her most of the day and observed the cheese operation.
September 3, 1995

I called Tatyana, my interpreter, and asked her to accompany me to Tsarkoe Selo, Catherine the Great's summer palace. It was built in 1756. We took the Metro and then the train 15 miles south of St. Petersburg. The palace's sheer splendor and opulence were incredible. To me it was even more ornate than Versailles. The extraordinary amber room originally designed for the Amber Cabinet at Konignberg castle was presented to Peter the Great by Frederick-Wilhelm of Prussia. Surrounding the amber panels are gilded carved mirrors. There are 450 kg of amber in this room.

In 1941, when German troops took Tsarsko Selo, the Amber room was dismantled and stored. When the Nazi war machine crumbled and was driven out of St. Petersburg the panels were crated up and moved out of danger and then eventually returned.

The town of Puskin, which surrounds the Tarskoe Selo Estates, is one of St. Petersburg's most charming suburbs. It was renamed in Soviet times to honor Russia's greatest poet Puskin. In less than two centuries the Romanov Czars established not one but two suburban estates, Tsarskoe and Peterhof. Afterwards, whenever I asked myself why there was a revolution after 300 years of Romanov rule I could see clearly why. The rich were living in such opulence and the poor were starving.

September 4, 1995.

Tatyana met me at the hotel and we went to the dairy to discuss with Maria how much cheese she had produced and how much supplies she had left. We called deputy director Irena to find out where some stores were that carried our cheese. Tatyana and I visited several stores and got the impression that the storekeepers were not positive about the new product. The label on it was all wrong; it was called Moale which is French for curd. There really isn't a translation for cheese curd into Russian. The closest translation would be like our farmers cheese. There were no Russians in our organization that really had any idea how to promote and market new products.

September 5, 1995

I went to the office and had a meeting with Victor and Galina, Gennady, Irina and their accountant. We discussed future marketing strategy of this joint venture and my displeasure with their distribution and accounting. What disturbed me most was the lack of fiscal discipline in a startup company. After the collapse of communism many of the state stores were no longer in existence, so much of the food products were sold on the street in kiosks or farm markets. Many housewives shopping for food and basic necessities for their families found it very difficult because of their meager salaries. When all of agriculture was subsidized by the government food prices were so cheap. One lady said to me she could buy bread for her pigs cheaper than grain. Prices skyrocketed with inflation. After our meeting I went back to the hotel and Tatiana set up some Russian lessons. I made every effort to study and learn the language whenever I had a spare moment.

September 6, 1995
Went to the dairy I met up with David Messmer. He was another partner with International Food and Beverage Corp. He was in charge of juice production and we spent the day preparing juices for packaging.

September 7, 1995
I got up at 5 AM to leave for Novgorod with Victor, Maria and Georgi to go to a cheese plant that is interested in making our products. While Maria was making cheese Victor took me on a tour of the city. It is the oldest city in Russia. The word Novgorod in Russian means new city. It was first mentioned in 859 when it was already a major station on the trade route from the Baltic to Byzantium. There were many bronze monuments to the millennium of Russia (1862). I felt how fortunate I was to work here in Russia and at the same time be able to visit all these ancient historical places.

We returned to the cheese factory to help Maria make cheddar cheese curd. We had a meeting at the office of the Director to discuss problems in general. They tried very hard to get me to consider investing money into this operation. This plant was built in 1977 and they claim they took in 750,000 pounds of milk per day. Today they take in 75,000 pounds per day. This is so typical of the Soviet Union when they always boasted how they built the biggest plants. They were huge but there is so much wasted space. I asked why they were taking in so little milk, he said milk production in Russia has fallen by 60 to 70% and cow yields are very low. Under the communist system all food and agricultural industry was subsidized by the government and things were much simpler. He told me now he had to borrow money from the bank at a line of credit to sustain daily operations. I was astounded when he told me he paid in interest upwards of 60%. This was to cover hyperinflation. He seemed to have a certain mentality about borrowing this money, if they default it's my problem. He said, "I did not create this situation".

We tried the cheese Maria made which turned out very well, and made a few toasts with cognac. They really weren't interested in the cheese that she made. They were only interested in how much money we were going to invest in their operation. They were desperately looking for some foreign investments. Of course I explained I am only bringing my technology to make new cheese products. So everything was kind up in the air and the meeting ended.

We drove 200 km to St. Petersburg and Victor drove 85 mph. The vehicle was a Dodge van that we had shipped to Russia and he explained to me the difficulties they had with customs just trying to get this car registered in Russia. The highway was not the best highway and I ask him why he was driving so fast with such a vehicle that was quite old. He said, "It's more fun driving fast".

The next day I went to the dairy and had a meeting with Irene, Olga and Maria. They had produced cheddar cheese curd of rather poor quality and it is not selling as expected. They were cutting corners and not making cheese according to my specifications. They tried to make curd out of poor milk to cut their costs. Also the juice production was not consistent. Many production and personnel problems were discussed. It was apparent there were problems with leadership in the company. There was infighting and not coming together as a team. They need strong management who can set rules and exert authority and make consistent quality products. I began to realize that the Russian partners were in control when we returned to the US. I told them that in the US a startup company has to retain some profits in order to survive and grow. They seemed to think they could take the profits for themselves immediately, not thinking about cash flows.

That evening we went to the flea market and purchased some more souvenirs. There was a fast food restaurant called Carroll's. It was a joint venture between some Russians and Americans from the US. In fact there was a Carroll's restaurant near my community in the US. After I returned to the US I always went on my computer to read the English version of the Moscow Times and there was an article that said the Russian partners seized control of this restaurant and forced out the American partners. There were so many of these joint ventures failing that I was concerned about our joint venture.

September 9, 1995

It was Saturday and nobody worked at the plant. I spent the morning studying my Russian. I had tapes that I would play over and over and I began to retain some Russian phrases. I felt that I could walk around the city and do some shopping by myself using my limited language skills. It was a great feeling. Many Russians said they were amazed at my Russian. I told them that my Russian is very poor and they told me it's not poor, it's understandable.

Later that afternoon I met my translator, Tatyana, and went over to the summer gardens but they were closed so we just walked around the park because it was a beautiful day. Later when it started to rain we decided to go to a nice restaurant and have some wine. It was advertised for foreigners who wanted an American-style restaurant. I thought it would be nice to take Tatiana to an American-style restaurant. I couldn't believe how expensive it was. It really wasn't worth the price. Whenever they serve foreigners they feel they can charge much more.

September 10, 1995

Today was Sunday, another day off. I got up and made my breakfast and did some reading and packed my bags to move out of the Octoberskya Hotel and move in with David Messmer. John and Lou Tarr arrived to install a new pure pack machine to package juices.

September 11, 1995

Jim Shue arrived at the office and we had a daylong meeting at the dairy in their offices to discuss all the problems they were having.

September 12, 1995

We went to the dairy. Maria and I decided to make some mozzarella cheese. Pizza was getting to be very popular in Russia. They wanted a cheese that stretched like Italian mozzarella. We also made some gouda cheese and coated it with poly coat. This is a wax like substance to preserve it. I told her age the gouda for two months and about 45 degrees and assess the quality.

September 13, 1995

I went to the office and had a meeting with Jim Shue. Our Russian partners failed to show up so Tatyana and I decided to catch a taxi and then the boat to Peterhof. John Tarr was installing a machine at the dairy so we invited his wife Lou to join us.

Peterhof is probably one of the most popular attractions in all of Russia, often referred to as the Russian Versailles. It was Peter the Great who was inspired by the architecture in Europe to build this Imperial Palace. The most spectacular part of Peterhof is its fountains. Millions of visitors every year visit Peterhof. It comprises 64 different fountains and over 200 bronze statues which include the truly most spectacular Grand Cascade. It truly is an engineering marvel. The water runs by gravity from the Gulf of Finland. The grotto behind the Grand Cascade contains the enormous pipes, originally wooden, that fed the fountains. Peterhof is open usually from May till November. In the winter months pipes are drained to prevent freezing.

Like most of St. Petersburg suburban estates, Peterhof was heavily damaged by German troops during World War II. It was, one of the first to be reconstructed, thanks to the work of military engineers and over 1000 volunteers. Most of the state's major structures had been fully restored by 1957.

September 14, 1995

I caught a night flight out of St. Petersburg and arrived in Novosibirsk 6:30 in the morning. Lou and John Tarr accompanied me on the flight. He installed some packaging equipment and trained some Russians how to operate this machine. It was at the Siberian Milk Factory, formerly called Kirovsky Dairy. I was met by the general director, Victor Komasjk, chief engineer Alexander Scherbinin and Deputy Director Ivan P Micheev. I showed them the cheese products that we manufacture at my cheese factory in the states. They informed me that they were unable to make quality cheese because the milk was so poor. I said we'll give it a try if you'd like me to make some cheese for you. They said by all means, so they had a vat of milk ready for me, I added some rennet and culture to the milk, it would not coagulate. Come to find out the milk they gave me was milk that was returned from the store because it was sour. They pasteurized milk at high temperatures which denatures the protein, rendering it unable to make cheese. They did make a type of cheese out of this milk called tvorog which is basically milk that has turned sour and then drained in a milk cheese cloth like our farmers cheese. I was disappointed because I really want to show them how we make some of the cheese. They seemed pleased that they could learn the procedures and eventually start to make some cheese. I returned to my hotel that evening.

September 16, 1995

John and Lou Tarry and I took a walk around Novosibirsk and purchased souvenirs. At 11 AM the directors from the dairy took us on a tour of the city with their company car. We saw old log houses so typical of the architecture in Siberia. I was quite surprised that there are preservationists trying to preserve some of these earlier structures and the Old Russian Orthodox churches. Then we drove about 20 miles outside the city to one of the largest power projects in the world. We returned to the city and went to a restaurant where they prepared a huge dinner for us. Victor and Alexander said they have been unable to make any cheese in this plant because of milk quality. But this was a learning experience and we are optimistic things will improve in the future. This was a very difficult time during this transition to a free market. Everyone made a toast and they presented us with some going away gifts. .They told me you are the first Americans to visit our cheese plant and it was an honor.

I flew back to Washington DC and again had to report to Citizens Network to be debriefed. My report to Citizen Network basically was

1) It has been a year since I have shipped and assembled a pilot cheese plant in Russia for the production of American-style cheese

2) I believe we are the first cheese company in the US to accomplish this.

3) If it wasn't for citizens network and their funding and the money from International Food and Beverage Corporation it would never have been possible.

4) We tend to focus on the negative factors and problems
   a. Sanitation
   b. Solvency of company
   c. The buying power of Russian people
   d. Crime, bribery and corruption

I felt Jack Quatermous had changed their mind set by his firmness and assertiveness in regard to employee relations. The Russian response to our cheese was very favorable and they seemed to indicate they would spend money for quality cheese where they may not for other necessities or luxuries. Bankrupt industries are of no benefit to them or us as trading partners.

Pollution abatement programs are essential to American manufacturing concerns. This must be incorporated into the mind set of our new Russian entrepreneurs. The service sector is creating a multitude of jobs in America. It could be duplicated in Russia with a restructuring of its economy. In these new joint ventures I feel Russians are pressing for every advantage for themselves. It has to be a two-way street if Russia wants to widen these privatizations.

Illegal mafia type activities should be curbed. It's a drain on business and it tears at the social fabric of the nation. They seem to keep a high profile in the community and most Russians I spoke to find it deplorable. It is very difficult to find out who has authority. In the West we have a clear understanding of ownership, here it is not who owns the assets but who controls them. In the event of a dispute there is no legal or reliable course of action. In Russia it appears that some US businessmen are like carpetbaggers descending on a defeated nation. This is a suspicion that goes back to the Cold War.

Citizens Network extended their hand and thanked me for all my volunteer efforts trying to do my best and indicated they were willing to continue funding my work in Russia

May Day Parade in St Petersburg on May 1, 1995 for Russia to Vote
for Communism to Return to
The Russian Federation

1996 Boris Yeltsin Re-Election

May 1, 1996

On my next trip to St Petersburg I again stayed at the Octoberskya hotel. Today is May Day, a holiday in Russia. I called Dave Messmer at his apartment and we met at Nevsky Palace Hotel. There was a huge parade on Nevsky Prospect, many bands were playing. We went out on the street to watch the parade and take some photos. The streets were lined with people, many older citizens with nostalgia for the Communist days of social order and for them a better life.

At Boris Yeltsin's election Communist leader Gennady Zyuaganov was repeating his demands. Much of the media was controlled by Boris Yeltsin's United Russian party and it was very difficult for the Communists to get access to television. I sensed that the Communists might come to power once again because the people were dissatisfied with their new found democracy.

Boris Yeltsin could not portray a forceful image of himself. Many people thought he suffered from alcoholism. It was revealed that a team of Neurosurgeons were flown to Moscow to operate on Boris Yeltsin after the election. He also suffered from an unspecified neurological disorder that affected his sense of balance. This bizarre behavior of Yeltsin resulted from drugs given to him by his doctors which were incompatible even with small amounts of alcohol.

In July of 1996 Boris Yeltsin was re-elected as president with financial support from influential business oligarchs and defeated his Communist rival Gennady Zyuaganov. Most Russians at this point realized that they could not go back to the old communist method of governing. The older folks with this nostalgia of the Stalin era were no longer a force in Russia. This was the beginning of the demise of the Communist Party in Russia. I can always remember in high school when we got our first television set. We would always watch the international news and I always remember May Day in Moscow when they would parade all their missiles and military hardware through Red Square, with thousands of Russians looking on. My translator said to me, I was a little girl in the Young Pioneers, similar to our Girl Scouts. I was all dressed up with a flower in my hair marching through Red Square where thousands of people were looking at me and cheering. I was so proud to be a Russian and to this day I love to celebrate our holidays".

May 2, 1996

Dave Messmer and I realized today was another day off, nobody was working and many were still celebrating. We visited the wax museum which exhibits a display of Czars' statues in wax of early Russian history. We had lunch and visited some antique shops and local kiosks where they were selling Russian souvenirs.

May 3, 1996

We had a meeting was Jim Shue, Dave Messmer, Victor Bezilevich and his son Anton. They were having difficulty with accounts receivable. So much of our product was sold in kiosks on the streets of St. Petersburg. They would order cheese paid a first-time, establishing credit and we would extend them credit for a few weeks and they would disappear. My policy was from now on we would extend credit for one order but not another until the previous bill is paid. What happened then was someone would establish good credit with several shipments then would tell us we are opening four more kiosks and order four times as much product then disappear. There was no way that we could recoup our losses. We were getting to the point where 30% of our accounts receivable were uncollectible. I was really in doubt about the future of this operation. Nobody had any common sense on how to conduct a business or impose discipline. You could not rationalize with these people.

My wife Trudy was scheduled to arrive late that afternoon. Nickoli, our driver in charge of maintenance, picked me up and drove me to the airport to meet Trudy. I was surprised to see her waiting for me at the airport. The plane arrived 40 minutes early. This was Trudy's first trip to Russia to join me and she was very excited and anxious to see me. One can feel pretty much alone at an airport where few people speak your language. Also she had a six hour night layover in Frankfurt, Germany. Then she flew to Warsaw, Poland. When she boarded the plane for St. Petersburg in the morning they offered coffee and vodka. She was surprised that anyone would drink vodka instead of coffee for breakfast. I can remember when first flying from Moscow to New York the passengers were mostly Russians. It was a nine hour flight, for many it was their first trip to America and they were excited and drinking vodka. Eventually Delta Airlines forbid any alcohol consumption on board except wine or beer when a meal was served.

Our driver, Nickoli, studied English in school and he did quite well speaking English. He drove us around St. Petersburg pointing out all the historic sites and places we should visit. Jim Shue arranged for Trudy and me to live with Ludmila Tasayeria (Mela) and her mother in an apartment on Komisar Sirnova Street. This was a typical Russian apartment, very small but comfortable. She had a friend who was a playwright from Germany often visiting her. At her birthday party we had the most interesting conversations and at times it had to be interpreted in three different languages. He spoke German, we spoke English and Ludmila and her mother spoke Russian. Somehow we all were able to speak to each other because some of us were bilingual. It turned out to be one of my most enjoyable birthday celebrations.

May 4-5, 1996 Saturday & Sunday

Next morning we took a walk along Nevsky Prospect and went to the Church of Spilled Blood. Then off to the flea market to buy some souvenirs. Then we went to the Hermitage. At noon we met Tatiana at the metro station and took a train to Czar Zelo and Puskin, Sunday we visited Peterhof and returned to Mela's apartment and had dinner.

May 6, 1996 - Monday trip to Petrosavosk

I had meeting with Jim Shue. He wanted me to go with him to Petrosavosk where there was a cheese plant that was interested in making soft varieties of cheese packed into100g packages. We went back to Mela's apartment, had dinner and prepared for our trip to Petrosavosk. Nikoli picked us up to take us to the train station at 9:30 PM. for a night train with sleeping cars. We arrived at our destination at 7:30 AM. It was my first trip on a Russian train with sleeping berths. Petrosavosk was a city of 300,000 people with one cheese plant. We took a tour of the plant; it was very clean and modern. They examined all my cheese samples. I tried to put together a proposal for them to establish cheese production. We spoke for about two hours, had a short lunch and toasted our endeavors with vodka. Late that afternoon we drove out into the country to some of the smaller villages in the area. Then we traveled back to the railroad station for a night train to St. Petersburg. I never realized how convenient train travel could be in Russia especially trains with sleeping berths. There was always this relaxed, wellbeing with fellow Russian passengers who never experienced sharing compartments with Americans. A boxed lunch and refreshments were served and we used bathrooms on the train to wash, shave, and dress feeling refreshed for a meeting or work. Also, it saved hotel expenses.

Trudy and I had breakfast and arrived back at the plant at 9 AM to have a meeting with Gennady, Plant Director, about packaging cheese in the new plant which they hoped to construct in the near future. They wanted to purchase cheese from foreign countries to serve some of the high end supermarkets that were springing up in St. Petersburg. After our meeting Jim, Victor, and I were beginning to become very discouraged with this St. Petersburg operation. There were no constructive proposals as who was going to finance this operation and they had some very lofty ideas. I felt there was collusion by a few Russians to fleece as much money out of the Americans as possible. Where was the equipment coming from and who would set up this equipment, who would market this cheese? Was a large part of this operation going to be a financed by the Americans? Everything was so nebulous.

Thursday, May 9, 1996

We got up at 5 AM to catch a plane at 7:15 AM for Frankfurt Germany. We landed at 1:30 and had to wait one hour to rent an automobile. We studied our map and drove to Niedersissen, arriving that evening at Trudy's relatives. We spent several days seeing all the members of family in the nearby communities. Then we visited some old ruins and a fortress built in 1500 and destroyed by Napoleon. We also went to Trier and visited an evacuation site that was discovered in 1980. It was a complete foundation of a complex of homes and Roman baths. Trudy and I had a few more days to visit relatives and then caught a flight back to the US.

Trudy had an Aunt, Regina Loth, who lived in Germany whom I greatly admired. She passed away recently in her early 90s. She was an army nurse during the Second World War in Stalingrad. Whenever I visited her; she could still speak a few words of Russian. I wish now I had talked to her more about her years in Russia.

I often spoke to people in Russia about the Second World War. I was in grade school and remember my father sitting by the radio for the news cast because so many of our relatives were fighting in the German Army.

The Battle of Stalingrad was one of the most important battles fought during the Second World War. It was a decisive victory for Russia because it marked the beginning of the end of the German invasion of the USSR. It was one of the bloodiest battles ever and one of Germany's greatest defeats. There are so many statues and monuments in what is now called Volgograd.

Gen. Georgi Zhukov is the most famous and revered hero in Russia today who commanded Russian forces during the battle. Hitler ordered Gen. Friedrich Paulus to take Stalingrad and capture the rich oil fields in the Caspian Sea at whatever costs to German forces. The exact number of casualties will never be known. However it is estimated that the German army had more than 750,000 men killed, missing or wounded. Archives record that the Soviet army, by comparison, had 478,741 men killed, and 650,878 wounded. Civilian casualties are not well recorded. The Russians captured 91,000 German troops. Of these prisoners of war only 6000 survived to return to Germany. One Russian friend summed it up and said "Tony, it's all part of our history today".

St. Petersburg Cheese Plant Encountering Difficulties

The St. Petersburg cheese plant continued a few more years. I was always concerned about the prospects of this business ever becoming profitable. If an American wanted to succeed in Russia he would have to live in Russia and be there ever day in charge. The Russian partners did not have that mentality. Without a Russian partner you could not even open a business. We couldn't turn out a good cheese product with the poor milk supplies. There were so many obstacles.

I would estimate the American investors could lose several hundred thousand dollars and it would ultimately fail. Most joint ventures in Russia have failed especially in the small business sector.

Jim Shue the principal American partner returned to the US. I have never been able to make contact with him and Jack Quatermous died of a heart attack several years afterwards while I was working in Russia.

I have worked with many new Russian businessmen who were hard-working individuals, investing their savings and energy into a joint venture. Many feared of having everything confiscated when it became a profitable business. One way many new ventures were destroyed was through the Russian tax system. If one follows the tax code exactly, it would be impossible to be profitable and pay all your taxes. The police are controlled by the mafia that extends into corrupt local governments.

There was a great euphoria when communism collapsed in Russia. Many thought new markets would open up for consumer deprived Russians and great profits could come from these joint ventures.

Fighting Crime in a Russian Court System

The present Russian legal system is incapable of fighting organized crime. It's impossible for American businessmen to have his day in court. Russian courts are still reluctant to take any initiative to define any new laws. Even the Prosecutor General's Office has never shown discipline in conflict of interest cases. Clearly job security and personal safety of judges and enforcement personnel must be improved to settle these disputes.

International Food and Beverage Co. Failure 1997

It wasn't long before I received many negative reports about the cheese operation in St. Petersburg. I always had severe doubts about the future of the cheese plant ever becoming fully operational and a profitable business. This operation was designed to defraud a group of Americans who invested probably upwards of $300,000 and finally threw in the towel and left Russia permanently. My worst fears were confirmed in the early days after the collapse of communism. Many Russians were enamored with the idea of becoming entrepreneurs and wealthy, not realizing it takes years to build up a profitable enterprise with a lot of hard work.

These are very difficult times in Russia and most of the joint ventures failed. There was always this euphoria in Washington that Russia was becoming a democracy. Businessmen could open new markets and many western companies would come to Russia to expand operations in a country where the people yearned for more consumer goods. It will take another generation before Russia will become a country where investments will have a degree of success. Even in America 90% of small businesses never survive in the long term.

I had several requests to return to Russia to help Russian cheese makers. I said to myself I will never get involved with somebody building a cheese factory again in Russia. It was a real learning experience.

Western NY Peace Center & the American Soviet Friendship Society

My work in St. Petersburg was finished. I had joined an organization called the Western New York Peace Center. It is an organization that has been active for over 40 years promoting education on local and global issues concerning peace and justice. I believe it became activate during the Vietnam War and has been able to sustain itself and continue to thrive and grow.

For nearly 40 years the Peace Center has acted as a force for progressive social change in Western New York and beyond. There were many young people in my area and at universities that were opposed to the Vietnam War. Being a very conservative Republican, I always hoped that democracy would prevail and communism would finally meet its death knell. I served in combat in the Korean conflict, war is not pleasant. I would do anything or join any organization that promotes peace, especially after working in Russia and learning more about two different world ideologies and how communism failed the people of Russia. Good business attributes would promote peace and prosperity.

I met several members in the Peace Center who were interested in Russia and belonged to an organization called the American Soviet Friendship Society (ASFS). It was actually a group founded by the US Communist Party in 1943 to advocate Soviet views and politics and to try to promote peaceful coexistence by fostering better understanding of our differences. Their mission also was to promote cultural exchanges. The Council had consistently denied accusations that it was a pro-communist organization and claimed to be non-partisan. Therefore leaders and members opposed the Council taking political positions on controversial issues. The Council had asserted its political outlook on a number of issues by opposing the US invasion of Cuba, and war in Vietnam. Throughout the Council's history, progressive religious leaders and churches have strongly supported the work of the Council.

Since the fall of communism the purpose of this organization has diminished. Now most anyone can travel to the former Soviet Union. There seemed to be an emphasis now on bringing foreign investment and business people to Russia to set up joint ventures. I felt maybe I could make contact with Russians working in the agricultural sector.

A New Adventure in Russia

My work in Russia was reported about in a many newspapers locally. Consequently, I was asked to be a guest speaker at many community and fraternal organizations, churches and clubs. I spoke to the Clarence Kiwanis Club about our St. Petersburg cheese factory in Russia. Afterwards a man approached me about a Mennonite community in Siberia called, Neudochino. Its name translated into English means "unlucky village". They desperately needed a cheese factory to process their milk. The inhabitants were not allowed to leave their village until about 1975 when Brezhnev was the premier of Russia. They approached the American Mennonite Community for help. After I spoke to the Clarence Kiwanis Club, word reached the Mennonite Central committee in Akron PA that I had shipped a cheese factory to St. Petersburg Russia. They contacted Ben Falk in Canada. He called me and wanted to know if he could meet with me and hear about the cheese plant we put together in St. Petersburg and possibly building a cheese plant in Neudochino, Siberia. At that time Ben and his wife Erna were living in Neudochino.

History of Mennonites in Russia

Catherine the Great of Russia issued a manifesto in 1763 inviting all Europeans to come settle in Russia, especially in the Volga River region. German Mennonites responded in large numbers. Mennonites from Prussia later sent delegates to negotiate an extension of this manifesto. Many of them settled the vast uncultivated lands of the Ukraine. These people religious, frugal and hardworking emigrants where successful farmers. Catherine the Great desperately needed these people to develop these agricultural lands and provide the food for the Russian people. As an inducement to encourage immigration to Russia, the manifesto offered the following rights and privileges to foreign settlers.

1) Free transportation to Ukraine
2) The right to settle in segregated colonies.
3) Free land and tax-free loans to establish their farms
4) Religious freedom and the right to build their own churches and schools
5) The right to self-government
6) Exemption from military service.
7) The right to leave Russia at any time

These rights and privileges offered a chance to thousands of people immigrating to Russia from the Germanic states and principalities of central Europe for a better life. All regions in Germany lay devastated and poverty was widespread from the Seven Year War that ended in 1763. Many Germans also immigrated at this time to other lands including North and South America in order to start a new life.

Russia was the first country in Europe to abolished serfdom and in 1865 allowed the serfs, not to own land, but to possess land where they could raise food and sell it on an open market. Actually this was at the same time that Abraham Lincoln issued his emancipation proclamation which freed the slaves. In Russia, many of these people were very industrious and self-motivated and became very proficient at farming. At that time, much of Russia's food was produced in the Ukraine. They also supplied much of Eastern Europe. Thus Ukraine was labeled the "Bread Basket of Europe".

When Joseph Stalin came to power in the early 1920s he embarked on his (NEP) New Economic Policy. His five-year plan initiated a total nationalization of the economy. Agricultural collectivization began in the Ukraine. The government took peasant's belongings including cattle, land and personal property and set up collective farms known as kolkhozes. Many more prosperous farmers called "Kulaks" (means tightfisted in Russian) resisted and were exiled, imprisoned or executed. The government Council of ministers established production goals. These quotas were set so high that it they were impossible to meet. Every peasant was allocated a small plot of land where he could produce food for his personal use. If the quotas on the collective farms were not met, everyone had to provide food from his private lot to make up the quota. The authorities would come in and confiscate the food and consequently many starved to death. It was government imposed genocide. It is estimated that over one million Ukrainians lost their lives through actual starvation. This broke the back of the nationalistic Ukrainian resistance. When I was working in the Ukraine they often spoke about this great injustice.

Many of these people were exiled into Siberia and many others left in search of a better life. By early the 1930s over 90% of the agricultural land was collectivized as rural households were forced onto collective farms with their meager belongings. Competition was suppressed because controlled prices were unrelated to supply and demand. Supply of consumer items fell into chronic shortages forcing customers to stand in endless lines. My translator told me her mother would stand in line for milk for her baby sister. When she came home from school she would take her place and her mother would prepare supper. This all was in the late 1980s. US president Reagan increased our military budget, proposed the Strategic Defensive Initiative (Star Wars), intercontinental ballistic missiles and all the new technology associated with modern warfare. Russians were competing and they couldn't finance their economy. I can recall when the price of crude oil was only $10 a barrel when I first started working in Russia. Communism was coming apart at the seams, crashing down under its own weight It was often stated in our news that Russia had a poor harvest which compelled them to buy grain on the world market from Canada, New Zealand and even the United States. When I was working in Ukraine and southern Russia, I couldn't believe how rich the soil was. It was black, and the top soil was 2 to 3 feet deep. The weather was very warm, even palm trees grow in the Caucasus around the Black Sea. What actually happened was that the government couldn't come up with the huge subsidies needed to sustain the farms. For instance, there was only one combine factory in Russia where thousands of people worked. When a combine broke down in the Ukraine it would take two months to get the parts. They grew barley, wheat and grains which were harvested in October. However in November, it snows and parts for the combine hadn't arrived. The grain could not be harvested. People who worked on a collective farm were not really responsible, they didn't own the farm.

Lawrence Klippenstein

Lawrence Klippenstein, Mennonite historian and author, contacted me by email and telephone when he found out through Ben Falk that we were building a cheese factory in Neudochino Siberia for a Mennonite community.

He shared with me numerous writings and facts about the history of this Mennonite region. Many of the people he met at his Mennonite conferences were people I directly worked with in the village.

I owe him a debt of gratitude for this information, knowledge and experiences within the Mennonite community. He was gracious enough to allow me to reprint his articles in my book to share with whom ever.

Following is the information Mr. Klippenstein submitted to me about the history of the Mennonites in Siberia.

Mennonites in Siberia

Part 1

By Lawrence Klippenstein

Slavgorod Mennonites Then and Now

The Omsk "Germans in Siberia" conference last June was a busy time so I could not get around to everything I had hoped to do there. One part I missed was a tour to the city of Slavgorod about a 10 hour drive from Omsk, after the sessions were over. A group of ten persons did go so I could learn some things from them. Most of them had come to look for traces of ancestors who once lived in the villages of what was once the Slavgorod Mennonite settlement.

That settlement was begun around 1908 by Mennonites from villages in the older Mennonite colonies, some from the Volga area and others from the mother colonies of Choritza and Molotschna. Oberschulz Jakob A Reimer was an important leader to help the settlers get started. They received a large tract of land lying between the city of Barnaul on the Ob River and the Irtysch River some miles to the west. At first the settlement was known as the Barnaul settlement because Barnaul was the largest city nearby. Eventually about sixty villages were founded in the Kulunda steppes as this area was known. By the early 1920s the total population of these new communities reached about 15,000 persons.

A major problem for the new settlers was the distance they had to travel when shipping products to market — 150 miles at first. The city of Slavgorod was then founded around 1910 by the Russian government about 15 kilometers southwest of the settlement and 160 kilometers south of the Trans-Siberian Railway.

When a branch of this line was laid in 1916 going south through Slavgorod, market connections for selling wheat and other produce like cheese and butter were greatly improved. Mennonites began to move to the new city almost right away. A number set up businesses which flourished in the years ahead, though that would change when the Bolsheviks took over Russia in 1917. Several Mennonite churches were established in the city even before the Revolution. A number of worship centers were also erected in the villages.

Among other things the Omsk conference group visiting Slavgorod stopped along the way at the former Mennonite village of Neudochino (some Mennonites still live there) about which I will write later on. The road to those parts is quite rough in spots but interest was high, and all went well. After a good visit hosted by the local Evangelical Baptist/MB church, the city tour of Slavgorod a considerable distance away yet, was introduced by a Low German speaking minister, Alexander Weiss. He is a pastor at the large congregation of Evangelical Baptists (unregistered) which is active in Slavgorod. He had given strong leadership to establishing new churches in the area in the 1990s. He told me they had sixteen smaller groups meeting in the area.

The Evangelical Baptist congregation which is now his main responsibility has constructed a large new church building in recent years. Many former Mennonites, especially those of Mennonite Brethren background, have become part of this congregation.

I had a pleasant chat with Alexander at the hotel where the conference was held. He spoke at some length about a yellow mill (gelbe Muehle) which remains even yet, a landmark of the community. It was to crush grain to make various products out of grain produced in the area. However before it was finished, the

Soviets took over and the structure was converted into the main prison of the area. Many locals, including Mennonites, were imprisoned and often then executed at a place further down the road which has an unusually large cemetery, even today. Members of the tour group joined Pastor Weiss in a moment of memorial, with prayer, to remember the suffering and sacrifice of life which once took place here.

Churches which registered with the government of that time promised to obey these regulations but unregistered churches persisted in carrying on the work of the church as they felt they must if they were to be faithful to God's Word. Pastor Weiss and other leaders who have had long experiences with Russian and Soviet government practices believe that a time of more repression and even persecution may be coming again soon.

After a luncheon at the big Baptist church, the group was taken to see furniture and a cabinet making factory downtown, they are owned by Isaaks and by Neufelds. Mostly church members are employed here. Someone noted that Mr. Neufeld had been away looking for markets for his products in Mongolia. It was clear that people believed in a future for the community of Slavgorod and the families of the church here.

When the Bolsheviks took over all of Siberia in the early twenties the settlements were organized to give them full control. Production of grain and other farm products soon dropped dramatically in German and other communities. When collectives were introduced, some farmers went to Moscow in 1929 to secure passes to emigrate. When they succeeded, hundreds of families sold everything and rushed to Moscow in 1930 to get out, also, if they could. Very few made it this time. Those who managed to escape almost all found their way to Fernheim in Paraguay. A book titled *Vorden Toren Moskaus,* recently republished in English, tells this story in detail.

Most were rounded up in their temporary Moscow homes and sent back to their home communities, totally impoverished, or into labor camps. Thousands of men were removed from their homes during the Stalin terror years. When they were released, after hundreds had died, many could return to their home villages which had remained relatively intact. Persecution of churches would continue for decades.

Some of the collectives were dissolved after the Communist regime fell. Some villages left the collectives to work as independent communities, though remaining organized similar to collectives within the villages. A small amount of the land has been privatized by now. A number of new church buildings, usually belonging to Evangelical Baptists have been built, or are under reconstruction. Most of the ethnic Mennonites emigrated from the Slavgorod area to Germany beginning around 1990.

It is almost certain that contacts with the Slavgorod settlement will be continued and increased through tours and other ways in the upcoming years. One such tour is scheduled to take place in May, 2011. Connections with families in western countries are increasing. It is assumed that more information about this settlement will then become available to those interested and connected to the story.

Mennonites in Siberia
Part 2
By Lawrence Klippenstein

Neudochino; a Mennonite Village
I did not plan, at the June Omsk conference, to go to the village of Neudochino, about a two-hour ride from Omsk to the east and somewhat south, but others in our group did. As I said last time, those who took the side trip to Slavgorod went by way of Neudochino because they had people there to see.

I did meet the pastor of the Baptist/Mennonite Brethren church there, Harry Sawatzky, chatting a while in the Ibis Sibir hotel where our conference took place. He had come to arrange a meeting with several conference guests, Richard and Hedy Braun, who had brought some goods from their home community in Ontario, to pass on to Harry and his congregation. I did have a few related things I hoped to send along too.

A number of years ago a Russian professor, Dr. Okhsana(?) Baranov visited the USA and met several Mennonite scholars who asked her for an article on the village when they found out she was familiar with the community. That article, published in a Mennonite journal helped us in the West to "discover" that village. It had been more or less hidden away from Western eyes till then because it was somewhat off the beaten track and tourists had not had a chance to visit the place.

Then MCC decided it would be a good thing if some volunteers were placed there to help the community in development and other ways. Two volunteers, Ben and Erna Falk from Ontario, chose to go out there to see how they could help. Their going out took place while my wife, LaVerna and I, were serving in Moscow as country representatives for MCC. Part of our work was to help the Neudochino volunteers settle down in the village for two years, and then give support to them when needed as the work progressed.

We made that trip to Neudochino from Moscow in late February of 1993. The temperature was about minus 25 Celsius, and the regions we travelled through for two days and two nights by train were snow covered all the way. We had sleeping cabins and travelled by a train called the Siberiak east ward on the Trans-Siberian Railway for hundreds and hundreds of miles to get there.

After we got to the western boundary of Siberia the countryside looked much like southern Manitoba or Saskatchewan in winter. Our plan was that I would stay a few days, meet community leaders and begin discussions of outlining somewhat why the Falks had come and what was needed to help them get started.

When we got to Omsk, the city of our conference in June, we unloaded the belongings and several Neufeld brothers, one of them George from Neudochino, took it all by car and trailer to their home village. The ride was quite pleasant with the weather cold but without blowing snow, and the main road quite passable.

In time we learned that Neudochino had been established around 1905, and indeed, later celebrated its centennial in 2005. Ben Falk returned for the occasion, and various officials took part in the ceremonies. He and Erna had learned that at its peak of development over 100 Mennonite families had lived in Neudochino – six hundred people or more. They were all farmers really and held a large tract of land in the area.

When it became possible to emigrate in the late 1980s, some of these families began to leave as did Germans in many other places in Siberia. They all headed for Germany if they could. Today only about thirty Mennonites families still live in Neudochino. Houses left vacant by people moving away were bought by other Germans, Catholics and Lutherans, or by Russians.

During the Stalin years, many fathers and others were sent into labor camps, often located in northern Siberia, and a number did not return. A monument to remember them has been set up in recent years.

We were also told that the community was forced to form a collective when the Soviet government took over. They became one economic body with four other villagers, all Russian villages, and it was said Neudochino consistently was the village with the highest productivity of the five.

When they asked to become independent around 1990, they were allowed to do so with one Heinrich Ens becoming the mayor of the village. He had been a leading executive in the collective farm and had many contacts in the area which became helpful (occasionally also the opposite) in developing as an independent community once more. They continued to operate as a cooperative, with a central office hiring all those who wanted work, and paying them a salary, very low by our standards. Women had their work, mostly with milking cows, while the men did the field work, and some had other occupations, like the Neufelds who ran a body shop.

In Germany Neudochino families who moved there tried to live close together if they could. Raunen was one community where a number of families re-established homes, found jobs, and began to attend churches even when they had not done so in Siberia.

The family of Rev. Gerhard Neufeld, long-time minister in Neudochino was a leading family of Neudochino. At first Gerhard would not hear of leaving, and would not give his blessing to those in his own family who did. Finally, when all had decided to go, they persuaded their father and mother to join them.

It was a very difficult time for Gerhard. He passed away recently, not ever having been able quite to adjust to his new homeland in Germany. It was our privilege to stay in their home for a while and to meet the family when we went out there in 1993. They were part of a so-called Kirchliche Mennonite congregation, a small group of 30 members or so.

This had functioned there for many years. The other congregation began as a Mennonite Brethren congregation and remains active even today.

When Ben and Erna first came, part of their work was to help in the work of these two churches where they could. Services were also held in nearby Russian communities. They also helped with teaching German and looking after a large orchard, as well as promoting projects like a cheese factory which was built later on, building a hog barn which did not become successful (it was apparently torn down for fuel after Ben left), and offering counsel and advice in various ways to help make the life of families a little easier in a very difficult environment

At the Omsk conference I was able, as I said earlier to have talks with a former resident of Neudochino, Heinrich Peters, a young man who married in 1991, then moved his family to Novosibirsk. We sense he hoped to help his parents (his father had been pastor before him) and also to become pastor of the church in Novosibirsk. Living conditions were difficult and supporting a family there was a big challenge.

Andre's own family found more support returning to Neudochino while Heinrich developed his pastoral work in the Novosibirsk Mennonite congregation. His gifts in music and preaching were significant for the congregation although living conditions brought continuing difficulties, which remain to the present time.

Neudochino, one might add, got its name from the man who sold land to the Mennonite pioneers who came to start the community. His name was Neudachin, which means "not happy". People have commented from time to time, that the name fitted the experiences of many families there over the years.

At present some things are changing, some families have set up productive private farms with help from Canadian friends. It is possible that the remaining Mennonites, at least the younger families, will discover new opportunities of making a living and carrying on church work at the same time. May God grant it to be.

Word arrived at the Mennonite Central committee in Akron PA that I put together a pilot cheese plant in St. Petersburg Russia. Ray Brubacker in charge of Asian Mennonite programs contacted Ben Falk. Ben and his wife Erma were very active in Mennonite work around the world. They spent two years in this Mennonite village of Neudochino. His goal was to build a cheese factory in Siberia to utilize the milk from their 800 cow collective farm. Over the Christmas holiday he returned to his family in Niagara-on-the-Lake in Canada. He called me to discuss the possibility of shipping a cheese factory from the US to Siberia. I thought to myself this would be a very difficult task. In St. Petersburg I actually moved into a cheese factory which had most of the necessary equipment for making cheese. I only shipped specific equipment needed to produce new varieties of cheese, a vat, curd mill, packaging equipment and necessary materials. In the Siberian village of Neudochino we needed to build the plant from the ground up. This project would be much larger in scope. What concerned me were the custom fees. Whenever I wanted to accomplish something the outcome was always predicated on some level of bribe.

I invited him to my home with but thinking I didn't want to get involved in another project in Russia. When we discussed building a cheese factory in Siberia with all US equipment sounded like a herculean task. I told him of the problems that I had with customs and the Russian government. Ben told me all I had to do was design a cheese plant and acquire the necessary equipment. The Mennonite Central committee would oversee this whole operation. Also, a Mennonite committee in Europe would be working in our behalf. The German government would pay all shipping.

The German constitution states that any person with German ancestry could return as a refugee. With the German unemployment rate reaching 10%, Germany was trying to do whatever they could to stem the flow of immigrants. They made an agreement with the Mennonites that they would defray the cost of shipping milk processing equipment from the US and pay custom fees. They were under the assumption, at least they told me so, that there would be no custom fees because the machines were considered humanitarian aid. The village consisted of about 1/5 German Mennonites and 4/5 were Russians.

The more I thought of this project and all the support the European and American Mennonite communities had pledged, I began to become excited about the prospect of developing a cheese factory so far away in Siberia. My wife encouraged me by saying that anyone who is so energized will succeed. Letting the moment pass would be a cause for regret. Consulting my contact list, first I spoke with Kevin King, resource manager in charge of all shipments to Mennonite communities around the world. I drew up a list of equipment. I needed a boiler; pasteurizer, separator, butter churn, and the list went on and on…

I never asked my suppliers for a direct donation; however I needed a reasonable price because the equipment was going to Russia to build a cheese plant which was desperately needed. I was amazed how people reacted with low prices, donations and well wishes.

When I explained to US-AID in Washington DC that I was volunteering to build a cheese plant in Siberia for a Mennonite community, they reviewed my past experience and quickly approved.

In 1962 President Kennedy established a US agricultural foreign aid program to promote farm development around the globe. In 1982 President Reagan noted that volunteer assistance enhances the security of the United States. The importance of security and development assistance program cannot be exaggerated. The United States had come to realize investment leading to peace and stability is far less costly than war and reconstruction.

The Task Begins: Assembling a Cheese Plant in my Back Yard in Corfu, NY.

I searched the country scrounging for used and new equipment. I had many conversations on the telephone talking to suppliers who could help me find the necessary equipment that I needed for our new cheese plant in Russia, My son Thomas had just graduated from Boston University and provided me with a computer and hooked me up to the internet. I cannot imagine what my telephone bill for all my calls to Moscow would have totaled without internet access. There was no internet in Neudochino but they did have fax machines. I would send an inquiry or question to my Moscow office; they in turn would fax it to Neudochino, Siberia. They would return a fax to Moscow and e-mail me here in Corfu. This was a tremendous help to me.

One does not realize that this equipment has to be interfaced with electrical systems in Russia. Our power generally speaking is 110/220 volts but 200/360 in Russia. We have 60 cycle and they have 50 cycle. When I purchased a boiler to produce steam all the controls were built for 110 volts so we had to install transformers to achieve the proper voltage. A cream separator rotates at 6000 RPM on 60 cycles. However, on 50 cycles per second it only spins at 5000 RPM. This will not separate cream from milk. What I did was purchase some of the equipment in Europe. I sent refrigeration equipment that requires a gas called R12 that is outlawed for environmental reasons here in America. We also needed all the stainless steel piping, sanitary pumps, vacuum equipment, pasteurizers and packaging material. Milk storage tanks and all the other incidentals had to be sized up and engineered to meet the design of this facility. The list goes on and on.

There are no hardware stores in Russia. Under the old communist system with its high level of bureaucracy everything was supplied by their planned economy. Many of the young people were heading to large cities in search of higher paying jobs. These were the younger self-motivated individuals so important to the future improvement of the village.

They had 600 pigs on the farm and they needed a quick means for making sausage and meat packaging. After I assembled all my equipment in the backyard of my cheese factory in Corfu in New York, the Mennonite Central committee in Akron Pennsylvania sent a container which is an empty truck body transported behind a tractor trailer. I hired special equipment and loaders to put all the equipment into the container and ship it to Akron Pennsylvania. The equipment was re-wired to run on Russian power and the boiler was converted from natural gas to propane. They said there was no natural gas in the village. One phase of my project was now completed and I breathed a sigh of relief. I felt better prepared to start the second phase, assembling everything. Meanwhile they kept me up to date on the building project. They actually had to build a building to house this operation. There were many phone calls and e-mail messages over a period of several months. In the back of my mind I always worried "What have I forgotten?"

ACDI -VOCA Washington DC
Michael Harve, - Country Representative from US
Vladimir Soldatenkov - deputy director in Russia
Irena Paisova - senior project coordinator
Tonya Nvozhilova - translator
Yuri Arkhipov - My personal driver

These people where so helpful and worked so hard to help me make this a successful venture. In Washington the office obtained my visa and provided me with a stipend. The Moscow office arranged my travels on trains and aircraft and would debrief me before I returned to the states. They arranged my hotel stays and registrations. When traveling in Russia there was still a semblance of the old days when a visitor's whereabouts was constantly monitored. Upon arrival I had to register with the local police department and state my length of stay and purpose for traveling and all destinations. All papers had to be properly stamped. If papers were not in order a fine could be levied

From Corfu to Neudochino Siberia
It was the fall of 1996. The Mennonite Central Committee in Akron Pennsylvania sent a 66 foot long container, a tractor trailer, to our cheese factory in Corfu, New York. Every cubic foot was carefully filled with equipment. We had to estimate how much room to leave for a butter churn, cream separator and meat packaging equipment which would be loaded in Germany. It arrived in Bremerhaven, Germany and was transported overland to Neudochino Siberia.

THE FOLLOWING ARTICLE IS REPRINTED FROM THE MCC NEWS
SERVICE ABOUT OUR SIBERIAN VENTURE

Unique Relief Arrives: MCC Sends Cheese Factory to Siberia

Emily Will of (MCC) Mennonite Central Committee news service sent me this
article.

Akron, PA —Mennonite Central Committee has sent everything from
soap to tractors to people in need around the world, but now
Mennonite Central Committee is sending something new: a cheese
factory.

The disassembled factory, plus boiler, is on the way now, making
its way from Corfu, New York to Neudochino in Siberia, Russia. With
its arrival and assembly, townspeople in Neudochino will be able to
make cheese from milk produced by their 800 purebred Holstein
cows. The project has its origin in MCC's placement in Siberia of a
retired farm couple, Ben and Erna Falk of Niagara on the Lake,
Ontario in January 1993.

Leaders of Neudochino, with about 700 people, many of ethnic
Mennonite background, had asked for workers who could develop
village businesses in an effort to keep young people at home. In the
past four years, nearly 40% of Neudochino Mennonite population
has immigrated to Germany.

"In 1993 when we met the Falks, we didn't know Russian
agriculture was descending into a crisis from which I have yet to
recover", said Walter Bergen, MCC country representative for the
former Soviet Union. "Ben and Erna have had that challenging job of
walking alongside Neudochino residents as they struggled to adjust
to post Soviet life".

Village administrators came up with the idea for a cheese factory
as a more efficient way of using the 10 tons of milk village cows
produced daily. Cheese can be held until transportation is available
to get to market; milk cannot. The village leaders approached the
Falks about the cheese possibility, who in turn took it up with MCC
administrators. A couple of proposals were considered but in the end
proved not feasible. That town was without its desired cheese factory
when the Falks completed their MCC assignment and returned to
Canada in early 1995.

In September 1996, they received a call from Neudochino leader
Andre Enns. "The village can't survive without some help, any help",
Enns told the couple. Despite the town's valiant effort to be self-
sufficient, the economy around it continued to crumble.

"The call galvanized us to action" Ben Falk said. A trip to MCC
headquarters in January didn't produce an immediate solution for the
Falks. But it did provide them with a lead. Someone mentioned

businessman, Tony Kutter, who had worked on a cheese project in Russia with the organization Citizens Network for Foreign Affairs. On their return to Ontario, the Falks stopped to see Kutter at his home in Corfu, New York. "Kutter's first reaction was we'll see, the more he thought about the project, the more enthusiastic he became. God was at work", Falk said.

Within weeks, Falk and Kutter had worked out a rough plan for assembling a basic low-tech cheese making operation, using a mix of new and used equipment. Ben's knowledge of the village along with Kutter's experience with cheese making proved a providential combination, Berman said.

The project then became like a pebble dropped into water. Numerous ripples were created and many people got aboard these ripples, The MCC ministries and staff found itself thrown into a world of new technology. They learned, for example, that a condensate return system means a feed water tank and pump. "I am becoming a boiler expert!" chuckled Kevin King MCC coordinator of material resources.

Jim Bonfitto of Shillington, PA, a boiler and burner service contractor agreed to re-tube the boiler and adapted it for liquid propane instead of natural gas. He hoped someone in Neudochino would be able to make future adjustments and repairs to the boiler. "Siberia is kind of out of our territory," he said.

MCC Europe purchased a used butter chum and cream separator that Swiss Mennonites had located and with the help of the Aussiedler mission organization Aquilla, transported the items to Siberia. Meanwhile, the Falks left final details for shipping the disassembled factory in the hands of Kutter and MCC Akron, PA administrators and left for Russia. They accompanied the new MCC workers Bill and Betty Peters of Penticton, B. C. who will stay in Neudochino for two years. MCC plans to keep personnel in Neudochino and the region to assist with ongoing development efforts.

Some villagers didn't believe the project would come to pass. But the skeptics were convinced when the cream separator and butter chum arrived from Europe. The next day Ben helped the village men pour a concrete floor in the former childcare center.

On April 25 the US equipment, from a huge boiler, large vats, and down to individual cheese hoops left the Baltimore port destined to Hamburg, Germany. From there they were to be shipped overland to Neudochino. In addition the German government had indicated it would cover freight costs to get all equipment to Siberia, contributing the funds to allow this approximate $46,000 initiative to be realized.

"MCC is at its best when we can enable volunteers, who have a great deal of practical experience, to solve problems alongside local partners, with creative ideas," Bergen said. This time a cheese plant happens to be that creative idea.

Arrival of a Container in a Village - 1996

There were numerous difficulties when the container reached Hamburg, Germany. The American transportation company would not allow their container to travel into Siberia. They had a fear that the container would disappear into some unscrupulous Russian hands. They had to unload the equipment and transfer into two trucks. It took 28 days to reach Neudochino because of many detours for safety. It was the autumn of 1996. The customs inspectors arrived and the nightmare began. I was informed that this shipment of a "cheese factory" was a total misrepresentation when we asked not to pay the customs fees. The inspectors said "you listed this as humanitarian aid. Humanitarian aid is food, medicine, clothing and so forth". They placed an $80,000 fine and they locked up the container. It was my intent to travel to the village while the equipment was being transported. The village workers were still completing the building and bringing in the electricity and water service. There wasn't much I could do until they resolved the customs dilemma. Ben Falk argued with the uniformed officers stating that we have paid all the custom fees and the equipment was ours. He was told by one of the village men not to get into a heated argument because they were writing down everything he was saying. Ben Falk said that was one time where he felt threatened and felt that his safety was being compromised. Andre Enns, at a meeting in Tatarsk, negotiated the fine down from $80,000 to $25,000. There was another meeting held in Moscow but I was never informed what transpired at this meeting. I received a call from MCC. They said all that equipment is now in the building. I asked "How did you resolve the customs problems and fees"? I don't know whether they were joking but they said we just broke the lock and took the equipment. I said "My name is on that document and I don't want go to jail in Siberia". They said it was all taken care of.

Meanwhile there was 1000 acres of barley that needed to be harvested so many of the workers were taken off the building project and put into the fields. I hoped I would stay in Siberia in the autumn to complete this project. There is a certain color to the landscape just like upstate New York where I live. I told them I would come after the Christmas holidays. When I returned to the US I reminisced about my childhood. I remember going to a one-room country school with outside toilets and no running water just like it was in the village in Siberia. I can always remember I was six years old when electricity came to our neighborhood. It was brought by Roosevelt's rural Electrification Program. They told me that Neudochino first received electricity in 1975.

When I was a child my mother had a huge garden and we were forever canning produce. We had several pigs that we butchered and made into sausage. Likewise in this village in Siberia everybody had a garden. It was always in the front yard of their homes. They had no lawns but these well-kept gardens were an attractive setting to their front yards.

Because it was in the autumn we were digging potatoes and putting them in root cellars underneath their houses. We burned wood in the early part of the fall. When it got very cold we would burn coal. I recall in the winter when I walked outside I could smell burning coal and its sulfides that these chimneys emitted. I always participated with numerous daily household chores like chopping wood and digging potatoes. Russians are so resourceful. As difficult as time was there was always plenty of food in the refrigerator.

After the work was done sitting down to a wonderful meal gave one a sense of satisfaction and good fellowship with the people I lived with.

I was under the impression that since Russia then had free elections that democracy would filter down into the communities and free elections would be held in all the regions. However, this was not the case. When President Putin was elected the Duma gave him the authority to appoint all the governors to the 89 regions (comparable to our states) in Russia. That would be like our president appointing governors of all the 50 states in America. The Communist Party was still pretty strong and active in Siberia, especially in the farm communities

One thing always lingered in my mind and left an impact on my memory. I told them my name is on that customs document and I don't want to go to jail in Siberia. My fellow coworkers at the cheese factory in Corfu, New York jokingly asked me why they sent me to Siberia. Did I screw up?

February 2, 1997

I arrived in Moscow. Everything was snow-covered. The temperature was 15°F and the sun was shining brightly. The children were playing in the snow, sledding, skiing and skating. Wherever I went I felt like I was a kid again because at home near Buffalo, New York we had snow, ice and cold winters. Everybody later asked me what it was like in Siberia in the winter. I said it was just like home near Buffalo. The driver for Citizens Network drove me to their office. Mr. Scott, US Country Representative, took me out to dinner and briefed me on my trip to Omsk then drove me to my apartment.

February 3, 1997

I left the apartment at 8 AM for the airport to catch a flight to Omsk. Aeroflot was the Russian airline under the communist system and had been broken up into smaller airlines. These planes appeared to be very old and storage had no doors just nets to keep things from falling out above the passengers. A four hour flight from Moscow took us eastward about one quarter of the way across Siberia. We arrived 5 PM their time in the city of Omsk. The temperature was 0° Fahrenheit. The infrastructure at this airport left a lot to be desired. I retrieved my luggage in a Quonset hut with no heat. There were wooden planks on ground to keep from stepping into the mud. I met Bill Peters and a driver who had a 4 wheel drive Jeep. We headed out to Neudochino on a highway that was built from Novosibirsk to Moscow. They have been working on this highway for the past eight years and were scheduled to be finished in 10 years. I often wondered how they would be able to keep this highway open in wintertime. My driver said "they don't plow but the wind sweeping across Siberia blows the snow off the road surface. " There is no need to salt these roads. They are straight as an arrow and you very rarely approach another vehicle from the other direction, so you can go 50 to 60 miles an hour on a slippery surface and feel comfortable. In all the winters I spent in Russia I never really experienced a snowstorm or a whiteout. It would snow for a short time and then the sun would be shining again. When the air is dry and very cold and the sun is shining brightly it lifts your spirits. If you dress warm you feel great.

We arrived in the village after dark. We went to Bill and Betty Peters' home where I lived while I was working at the cheese factory. Bill worked in sales in agriculture and was a Mennonite minister. Betty was a registered nurse for the village

Feb 4, 1997

I got up early the next morning and Bill and I went to the cheese factory. All the equipment was arranged in this facility as I had planned. The first piece we set up was the boiler. We had a different orifice placed in the burner assembly so we could burn propane. However, I did not realize the volume of propane the boiler would burn with an eight foot flame. So they decided to burn oil. This required them to adapt a Russian oil burner to fit the American Cleaver Brooks boiler. I can't believe how resourceful our Russian partners are. Another problem we had was the oil would not ignite when it was very cold. So we fabricated a pre-heater which surrounded the oil lines coming into the building with hot water. All modifications had to be done in house; you can't run to a Home Depot or a commercial supply house to implement your next plan. Actually, we made our own acetylene gas for cutting metal. We took what looked like a metal garbage can where we placed a large piece of carbon. We would clamp the lid on tight, run water into the container producing enormous amounts of acetylene.

We fired up the boiler and set all the controls manually. We had to have an operator sit in front of the boiler to change the settings as it started to produce steam. I was surprised at how long it took to get steam. One of our Russian boiler experts told me that were using Siberian oil which does not have the same number of BTUs (British thermal units) or heat content as European oil has. It is the way they refined the oil. Not an expert on crude oil I took him at his word and waited and finally the steam pressure went up to 100 pounds. It sure gave me a feeling of relief that with their resourcefulness they were able to make the heart of our operation successful.

I involved myself in all the physical, manual labor of putting this cheese plant together. I took up the job of setting up the cream separator and bolting it to the floor. I broke a bolt, thinking where will I find a replacement? My Russian colleague said "let's go to the machine shop" he'll make you one. The first thing the machinist asked me was this metric or is this one of those rare unorthodox threads you have in the US. It was a very antiquated machine shop but, they could make anything. I was very relieved when they hooked up the electric and we started separating milk. They were very anxious for some skim milk for their calves. Then we hooked up the butter churn and turned all the cream into butter.

Next we put together the refrigeration system. It was a walk-in-cooler that was broken down into sections and reassembled at the cheese plant. Now we had to hook up the compressors for refrigeration. We had two men from Kazakhstan who assembled the refrigeration lines and installed the R-12 gas. Our next step was to set up the pasteurizer and the agitator that goes above the cheese vat. Everything seemed to be coming along well. The electrical work and most of the plumbing had been installed. I guess it was better that we were building this cheese plant in winter rather than spring or summer when the man power was needed in the fields. We fabricated a culture tank which is a necessary step in making cheese. I was fortunate that we could now buy cultures from Europe made by Hanson Corporation in Denmark.

February 5, 1997.

I went to the plant early in the morning and was surprised to see the boiler up and running. All the equipment was in installed and running. We spent the whole day scrubbing and testing equipment and running hot water through our pasteurizer.

I spent most of the next day working with our lab technician, Tonya, training her how to do product analysis, butterfat tests and coliform counts on raw milk. I hand carried a microscope with me on the plane so I could show her how to do microscopic counts to determine the amount of bacteria in milk. She was a biologist and had previously worked in a hospital. She caught on very quickly. She had gathered together a lab including all kinds of glassware, hot plates and scales. This is a very important part of ensuring good quality cheese.

February 6, 1997

It was Thursday morning and the first milk arrived. We opted not to make cheese. Instead they decided to separate the milk for the calves and make butter out of the cream. We fired up the boiler, pasteurized the milk and cooled it down. Next we pumped it to an elevated tank which ran down by gravity to a sealing machine for both five and one liter packages. This was the only Russian piece of equipment in the cheese factory.

Our Westphalia separator ran very well and did an excellent job of separating the cream from the milk. I instructed Lydia how to disassemble the separator for cleaning and reassembling it. I checked out the pasteurizer and the recorder. Legally pasteurized milk has to be heated to 145° for 30 minutes. They had a clock that recorded the time, however it was inaccurate. We found a clock repair man named Stefan who adjusted the clock and after that it seemed to work perfectly.

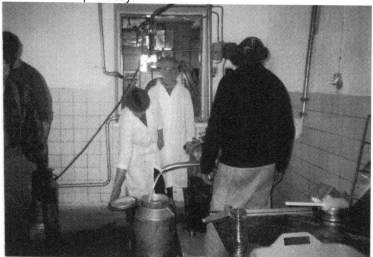

First Cheese Made in Our Siberian Cheese Plant

February 7, 1997

Arrived at the cheese plant and they had the milk ready for us. We pasteurized it and put into the cheese vat. We made about 300 pounds of cheese. First it appeared that we had no acid development but it ripened quite fast after the cheese was in the press. Cheese making is an art. In different parts of the world it seems to work differently so we have to develop a technique that works for you. The milk had a rather distinct farm odor which came through into the cheese. I tried to explain what needed be done on the farm. On US farms good ventilation is required. Cows generally give off a lot of heat and cattle like it cool. In Siberia with severe sub-freezing temperatures barns are closed up tightly. This can be overcome by keeping them very clean. My plan was to address this issue with everyone on the farm. Most of the people in the village were quite satisfied with the cheese that we had made.

February 8, 1997

We took our cheese out of the press, and cleaned our hoops and vacuum-packed our cheese in cryovac bags. It was a Saturday and is considered a non-work day. We went to the local school and borrowed some cross country skis. Bill, Betty and I went on a 5 km trek with our skis to the trans-Siberian Railroad tracks and watched the train go by. It travels from Moscow to Vladivostok and takes seven days. I will always remember lying in bed at night with frost on the windows listening to the Trans-Siberian railroad traveling near our village.

The temperature was about 5°. We were dressed warm and experienced no discomfort. We returned about 4 PM and went to banya. (A community bath house). It is a Russian tradition to go to the banya. After all it was the only place to bathe. The village banya was open all day Friday for men and all day Saturday for women. Many of the village people would turn out just for the friendly and neighborly atmosphere to socialize, drink vodka and tea.

Banya - Russian Bath

People from the centuries past and present not only washed there but used it for religious ceremonies to heal when they got sick, women gave birth and young couples found seclusion. Spend a day in one of Russians baths and you will sweat in the steamy bath and freeze in an icy pool of water, enjoy birch leaves (Venik) used to massage you with very warm water. But, after walking out of the banya, feeling 10 years younger with smooth skin like a baby you will promise yourself to come back.

Many villagers in Russia have a bathhouse, usually some way off from the rest of the houses in the village. There were also communal baths where men and women would sit steaming themselves and beating one another with birch branches and maybe even rolling together in the snow.

Peter the Great attempted to stamp out the idea as a relic of medieval Russia. He encouraged the building of western bathrooms in the palaces and mansions of St. Petersburg. But, despite heavy taxes on the banyas, noblemen continued to prefer the Russian bath.

Going to the bathhouse often was, and is, regarded as a way of getting rid of illness. It's called the "People's First Doctor" (vodka was the second, raw garlic the third). There were all types of magical beliefs associated with this folklore. To go to the banya was to give both your body and soul a good cleaning, and it was the custom to perform this purge as a part of a ritual. A banya was a place for a ritual pre-marriage bath and for the delivery of babies. It was warm and clean and private. The bathhouse was a steam room where heat came from heated stones. Humidity is added by throwing water on the stones. A vital part of the ritual was a leafy bundle of birch or oak twigs used for a body massage.

Garlic can also be a healer. I recall vividly on one of my trips to Russia flying from Buffalo to New York's Kennedy airport then boarding a flight to Moscow. Then catching a few hours of sleep and boarding a flight to Krasnodar. When I arrived I was picked up by my host and his body guard. We stopped at a restaurant and he wanted to a toast my arrival. I was suffering from jet lag but I was on a high because this was a new venture in southern Russia near the Black Sea. We toasted my arrival with vodka. I got very sick when I arrived at his house. His wife immediately said you go down to the Banya and I have a remedy for you. You'll go to bed and you'll wake up fresh as a daisy. She diced up a whole garlic, put it on a tablespoon and gave me a glass of water and told me to swallow it. I first chewed it and it burned my mouth. She quickly informed me not to chew it but to swallow it with water. I went to bed and felt great the next morning and now I really believe garlic is great medicine for what ails you.

Many times after we went to a banya we would all go into a separate room. We would all wrap ourselves tightly in Turkish towels. The women would bring some tea, the men would drink some vodka and we would sit there and had a nice comfortable warm atmosphere and just socialize. It was a great way to wind down after a difficult day's work.

I lived in Bill and Betty Peters house which had no inside toilets. It did have running water and a wash basin to wash hands, face and shave. Many of the village residents had inside toilets but some opted not to have this convenience but had an automobile. One rarely saw an automobile on the streets in winter. There were no paved streets in the village. It was something to get used to in the freezing cold weather, to go to an outside toilet especially when you have to get up in the middle of the night.

February 9, 1997

Today was Sunday, the day of worship in the Mennonite community. After breakfast we all went to church. I really enjoyed my time in a Mennonite church. They sang songs in German; however, it was Plautdietsch which is almost impossible for me to understand. I can understand German when they speak High German. Of course everyone here could speak Russian. It was a surprise when we were in the middle of a song and they switched over to Russian. I would ask why in the middle of a stanza they started singing in Russian. Well, they said when many Russians entered the church they knew they didn't understand German so generally, they switched to Russian. We also went to a Sunday evening service.

In the evening we went with Hans and Sarah Pankratz house for service where Bill Peters gave the sermon. Hans and Sarah invited all of us to their house after the service for coffee and dessert.

I highly cherished these invitations. I would always initiate a conversation about life under Communism in Siberia. The communists would not allow them to practice their religion openly. They would hold a religious service in their homes. They told me how often KGB deputies would patrol the streets at night. It was easy to look in the window. If you are holding a Bible or a songbook there would be a knock on the door inquiring what were they doing. They have been repeatedly warned to discontinue religious practices.

Marie told me when she was a schoolgirl, on Christmas Eve the family got together and conducted a prayer service and sang songs. Of course there was school on Christmas day because under Communism Christmas was not a holiday. The teacher asked everyone what they did on Christmas Eve. Marie was so excited she told the teacher that her family had a prayer service and exchanged small gifts. She was reprimanded. She had to stand outside the door of her classroom the entire day. This was a mild punishment, but to a child it was very humiliating.

Gerhard told me that his father took an unauthorized bag of grain from the farm so his wife could bake bread for their eight children. Because he was not a favorite of the Communist hierarchy in the village he was sentenced to prison (Gulag). His wife would write letters to him weekly but there was never a reply. This was not uncommon under Stalin. Life did improve under Brezhnev. When he was premier they received a letter from the Soviet ministry that stated "your husband has been unnecessarily executed" and all the letters were returned to her unopened. For compensation she now receives a free trip to Moscow once a year. "I don't go to Moscow because it is the most expensive city in the world. My pension is only $50 a month if I receive it". I would just sit and listen to stories in stony silence. Everyone could tell many stories about their family experiences.

I told them when I was a soldier in Korea 1953 I could vividly remember when Joseph Stalin died and people wept in the streets of Moscow. I asked if they had the same reaction. They said we put spit in our eyes before we went out into the public to demonstrate our sorrow.

In Stalin's day, before the collapse of Communism, one had to be very careful engaging oneself in a conversation about Gulags. I recall on one of my trips to Samara my interpreter was a very fascinating older lady who worked as a translator long before the collapse of communism. She arranged a unique opportunity for me to visit Stalin's bunker. It was a long elevator ride deep underground. He had living quarters and an office equipped with a telephone in case of a nuclear attack. They actually let me sit at his desk with my hand on the telephone to alert Washington about a potential nuclear attack and take a photograph with my camera. They said "this will be a great souvenir to show your grandchildren someday". They also told me about Winston Churchill's and Franklin Roosevelt's bunkers during the war. I remember this Russian guide spoke German. I speak enough German so didn't need my translator. Many educated

Russians studied German because of the Second World War with Germany. President Putin speaks excellent German. He spent the early years of his service in the KGB in East Germany, their most prized satellite.

It had just been open to foreign visitors but only to special VIPs. I do not consider myself a special person with VIP status but I am sure I was a favorite because of my work in Russia in the agricultural industry which is not politically controversial. I ask her if she was an English interpreter under the communist system, "did you work for the KGB"? Her answer was of course we had to report and document everything we discussed, where we went and what information she obtained in our conversation. This was just a normal requirement of any translator.

On one of my many evening dinner invitations I would bring up the subject about life under communism, gulags and its prisoners. Mennonites are conscientious objectors and they choose not to serve in the military. During the reign of Catherine the Great she honored this decree. Years later they were told if they wished to remain conscientious objectors they would have to work in the forestry industry in the far north.

Gerhard also mentioned member's families taken away to a forced labor camp on the Solovetsky Islands, situated at the White Sea in the far northwest of Russia. The secret police took over a Monastery on these islands and turned it into a brutal prison camp. The Communists considered these people political prisoners. By 1930 the prisoners of Soviet Solovetsky Camp began to be used as conscripted labor working in the forestry industry, chemical industry and paper production. Most never survived the harsh treatments and conditions to return to their loved ones.

Gulag

The Gulag system was a network of forced labor camps that, at its peak, consisted of 400 official prisons that held millions of inmates. Established in 1919, the system really did not flourish until the 1930s when Stalin used it with extreme regularity. The Gulag system is believed to be responsible for millions of deaths. That is more than the amount of Americans that have been killed in all wars combined. It is truly a gruesome part of history that has repeatedly been overlooked or ignored. I was in high school at the time and I thought this was mostly propaganda until I heard these stories. Many of these prison inmates were nothing other than common criminals. But by the Stalin era the prison population began increasing when citizens did not subscribe to his political, religious and economic directives.

Surrounded by walls of barbed wire, the camps were secretive and conditions were extremely harsh. Prisoners received inadequate food rations and insufficient clothing, which made it extremely difficult to survive the bitterly cold winters and the long working hours each day. Prisoners were often not told why they had been arrested and most were not allowed to ever see or hear from their loved ones. The guards also abused inmates, and as a result the death rate from exhaustion and disease in the camps was high. If prisoners were not killed working on one of the many dangerous social projects, they were killed in the camps by sickness, cold, or starvation.

Stalin used the vast amount of prisoners to his advantage. Turning the gulags into virtual slave camps, prisoners completed huge projects in building of canals, railroad lines, hydroelectric stations and hundreds of roads and industrial complexes in the highly remote regions of Siberia and northern Russia. Prisoners were also used to extract coal, copper and gold from dangerous mines and in the lumber industry in the vast Siberian forest. Stalin constantly increased the number of domestic projects which increased the need for more prisoners. The secret police often monitored people's activities and if you expressed a view not consistent with communist teaching you were arrested and told to gather your immediate belongings. Wives and children never saw them again. Hundreds of thousands of men were lost and never heard from again.

Gulag entered the world's consciousness in 1972 with the publication of Alexander Solzhenitsyn's epic history of the Soviet camps, The Gulag Archipelago. From the early days until the death of Joseph Stalin in 1953, some 18 million people passed through this massive prison system. It is estimated that 4 1/2 million never returned. The Gulag was not just an economic institution; it also became a country within a country, almost a separate civilization, with its own laws and customs. The vast array of Soviet concentration camps was rivaled only by the Holocaust.

A Pulitzer Prize winning book called Gulag: by Anna Applebaum, is the most interesting book I have read on this subject.

February 10, 1997
I arrived at the cheese factory and we cut the cured cheese into 10 pound blocks. We vacuumed packed cheese and boxed it up. Lydia and I packaged the cheese curd. She then cleaned the separator and the packaging equipment. After that I showed Tonya more lab testing procedures, mainly running milk butterfat tests, cream tests and moisture tests.

In the evening I went to the barn to get a milk sample directly from a cow so I could run a standard plate count and determine the degree of bacterial contamination of the sample. I brought with me some sanitizers and I thoroughly cleaned the cow's udder and took a warm dry cloth to dry it. I wanted to make sure it was absolutely free of bacteria when I took the sample. Milk from a cow's udder is practically sterile. However, milk is an excellent media for growing any kind of bacteria, especially as it passes through unclean equipment. When I ran the test the result showed it was very low bacteria count. However, when milk reached the plant it had a high count. The next thing we did was take line samples from the milking machines, to the pipeline, to the bulk tanks, the trucks that haul the milk to the cheese factory and then in the vat. I wanted to demonstrate how we can trace where the contamination was coming from. We determined the problem was in the milk pipeline.

It was very obvious that the glass pipelines were not clean. Most pipelines today are stainless steel but at least with glass you can see unclean surfaces. However this was a problem that we were unable to solve because of financial difficulties. To properly clean pipelines requires caustic and acid cleaners and very hot water. The hot water heaters had several broken elements which rendered them useless to clean these pipelines. It was something we had to live with the best we could. I found that making cheese right after the cows were milked, before bacteria increased dramatically. We could pasteurize it and make it into cheese and come out with a fairly decent product. In my budget I had $300 for a translator. They spoke German on this farm, a Mennonite dialect, which Bill Peters could interpret and translate for me. Of course sometimes they spoke High German which I could understand. He would not accept a $300 payment for translating services so I donated it to the farm for new heating elements for the hot water heaters.

February 11, 1997

We went to the cheese factory and cut muenster into the 6 pound loaves and salted them. Tonya ran a moisture test. It was 46% which was in the range what muenster cheese should be. After that we made our first run with our new butter churn. We made about 100 pounds of butter from cream which was slightly sour. This has been a practice in the United States for many years. People were accustomed to butter made from sour cream. I remember my father made sour cream butter back in the 40s and he would add some neutralizer to reduce the acidity and come up with a very good product. Today we pasteurize the cream immediately after separation which we intend to do in our plant here in Neudochino. I trained Lydia and Tonya how to rinse the buttermilk from the butter with clean water and how to work moisture into the butter. If this is not done when you spread butter on bread you will notice small droplets or beads of water which is not desirable. We packaged butter in 40 pound containers put them in a cooler. The following day we cut it into consumer sizes pieces.

Late that afternoon we went to the town hall. I had a poster from Cornell University on the technique of making good milk and had it translated into Russian. Returning to the cheese factory we tried to prepare a slide with iodine on a sample of raw milk for the microscope. The microscope I carried on the airplane along with the methylene blue dye stain to make bacteria visible under the microscope. I didn't realize the blue dye was highly flammable. The airport authorities took it away from me. So I had to experiment with iodine and I finally figured out how much iodine we could use so we could read the slide.

That evening I went over to Tina Steffens and she had prepared a Russian lesson for me. I took every opportunity to try to learn as much Russian as possible and enjoyed going over there. She was wheelchair bound and enjoyed teaching Russian. I was quite saddened a few years later to learn that she had passed away.

February 13, 1997

Today I traveled to a village called Kavaloria. They had a cheese factory there that was shipped from Denmark. It was put together and put on skids and reassembled in the village. Tanya and Vaughn Inns traveled with us. He's the brother of the director of village, and he would eventually be in charge of the cheese factory in Neudochino. We just wanted to share ideas and find out as much as possible about where they buy their cultures and the cheese that they were making. Unfortunately they were not making cheese at the time because of the lack of milk supply. It was not uncommon to dry up cows in the wintertime because of a lack of grain and hay for the animals. After a cow is bred and has a calf, it usually will produce milk for about 300 days. Then the cows are dried up. They have to be rebred to induce them to produce milk for their calves. It can be arranged to have most all of your cows dry during the winter months. This was the practice also in the United States many years ago. Back in the 30s my father only made cheese every other day in a winter time. Most of the cows would freshen in the spring and produce the most milk in June. We did have a great exchange of ideas. They did give us some calcium chloride which helped coagulate the milk especially when it is low in solids and proteins. They also gave us some lab supplies. Late that afternoon we returned back to Neudochino. The trip took several hours. In my community in upstate New York I can leave my village in Corfu and travel to Rochester and go through half a dozen villages. In Siberia when they say we're going to a nearby community you may drive 100 miles and see no sign of life or a village. One really gets a grasp of the vastness of Russia and Siberia.

When we got back to the Neudochino we took the cheese out of the press and put it into refrigeration. We had a problem with our cheese cutter so we loaded the equipment up and took it a machine shop. That evening we put together our posters for making quality milk which had been translated into Russian.

February 14, 1997

After morning milking we had a meeting with all the workers in the dairy barn. We discussed every facet of the operation and went over all the points on our educational posters indicating how to make quality milk. We had taken line samples so we could indicate where most of the problems were with contamination. We were able to locate some cleaning supplies and we attempted to clean the glass pipeline. Again our problem was we just couldn't get the water hot enough, but did the best we could. If we could have taken the pipeline apart we may have been able to clean them by hand. However, these lines were connected together with tight rubber couplings. The way they function is a huge vacuum pump creates a vacuum in the pipeline and sucks the milk from the milking machine to the bulk tanks for refrigeration. If we disconnected any couplings the possibility was that it might be impossible to create a vacuum in the pipeline if these couplers started to leak. It would be a catastrophe if you could not empty the milking machines when you are milking 800 cows. This is something they will have to correct in the future. They judged the cheese they were making was of good quality. By US standards I did not want to criticize when I did not have an answer as to how we could improve the conditions at this farm because of the lack of money to upgrade the system. First things first, as time goes on it will get better.

Many of the older workers said they were aware of the problems. They reminisced about former times when everything was taken care of by the state and was not the responsibility of individual employees. I was always truly amazed and astonished is to their resourcefulness. At times I was worried about the future of this village because so many of the Mennonites leaving to go back to Germany. They were usually the self-motivated hard-working families. Many of these Russians had German ancestry who returned to Germany and encouraged other families to join them.

What I found distressing and troublesome was the fact that some of the people I was training to manage the cheese factory were studying German. I thought they were practicing their German in order to converse with me in German instead of Russian. But their intention was that at some point they would join their fellow Mennonites who had immigrated back to Germany. The German government was tightening up on their refugee status mandating a certain level of proficiency in German. For emigrants they were guaranteed certain amenities which would be a vast improvement in their lives. I never realized how big a German enclave existed within the Soviet Union until I did some research.

Saturday's Feb 15, 1997

We made 2000 pounds of milk into cheddar cheese curd today. We use less culture and we used calcium chloride. This made much better cheese. The calcium chloride helped coagulate the milk. This milk had low solids because many of the cows have been milked for years and needed to be culled out of the herd. The acid development in the cheese was proper. This cheese was made by Vaughn and Tonya. The motor on our curd mill burned out and we had to cut the curd by hand. We finally finished at 5 PM. I went home and went to the banya for a bath.

Sunday, February 16, 1997

We went over to the cheese plant took and the pressure off the cheese press and put the cheese into the cooler. We went back and had breakfast and then got ready to go to church. After church we came home and had dinner and then we took a Sunday rest. Afterwards we went cross-country skiing. We passed the horse stalls where they had about 40 to 50 horses. The two men who were in charge just left the village and returned to Germany. They had taken such pride in their animals and even had troika races with neighboring villages. This was an event that was fun to see, three horses pulling a sled over a very icy surface. I never knew that horses love cold weather and they were always outside. In the summertime horses always look for shade to escape the heat. We are all saddened by the fact that the time may arise when they would slaughter the horses because of the economic conditions in the village and nobody to take over the responsibility. We returned home for lunch before returning for an evening Mennonite service. A neighbor also had their own horse and sleigh and invited us for a sleigh ride. It was so symbolic of a Russian winter; dressing up warm, the ladies in their fur coats, the air very crisp and riding through the birch forests of Siberia. We returned home to some hot tea and played some cards.

Monday, February 17, 1996

The temperature was above freezing. It felt like a small heat wave. We went to the cheese factory and started to make muenster cheese again. We packaged last Saturday's cheese and made unsalted butter. I think the cheese is getting better as we make a few changes and encourage the farm people to be more careful about sanitation. After the cheese was made we packaged the butter and then the cheese curd into 6 ounce packages. Bill and I washed up some of the equipment ourselves that wasn't as clean as we would have liked. We were running out of Cryovac bags but Vaughn had some material we could make bags out of. I hope it will work. We need material with an oxygen barrier. This type of material prevents oxygen from entering the bag. It prevents cheese from becoming moldy. In addition, in our US plant we flush bags with nitrogen which is an inert gas. Mold will not grow in the absence of oxygen. This is another step in packaging I want to introduce in the Neudochino plant. All in all this had been one of our better days. Many of the workers are impressed with our progress. Tonight I am going to the farm to get some samples of milk so I can test for quality. Hans and Sarah Pankratz invited me over for dinner. These dinner engagements were always enjoyed because of the lively conversations that followed.

Tuesday, February 18, 1996

We made cheddar cheese again today and packaged Monday's cheese curd. It was an excellent cheddar cheese. I found out why acid development was always late because slabs of curd cooled off and when I saw what was happening I would turn a little steam on in the bottom of the vat to warm the curd. This produced a proper acid development which is so essential during the curing of cheese.

That day we experienced a problem with the electricity. There was something wrong with the current coming into the building. Our motors both Russian and American were overheating. It was quickly resolved by one of our electricians from the village.

I went to the farm to get another milk sample right from the cow and from our freshly packaged milk. I tested it to determine the bacteria count. We package milk for consumer use and I wanted to show them how much longer the shelf life of milk is when it is packaged with a low bacteria count. Rules and regulations in Russia was that it could only have a three day shelf life.

Many stores did not have proper refrigeration. When I said that we have a two week shelf-life on our milk in the US they we appalled. Every one replied I would never buy milk that old. I don't care how good you think your milk is. I want fresh milk. When I was so adamant about improving our quality they would often respond "Hey, there's nothing wrong with our products". The milk was packaged in one liter bags. This type of packaging was never acceptable to consumers in the US. You have to empty this bag into some container at home because it is impossible to pour liquid out of a bag without empting the entire bag. However, it's much more inexpensive to package the milk this way.

There was no competition under the communist system so quality wasn't important, quantity was important to fulfill quotas. When I first started coming to Russia if someone wanted my expertise and invited me to his cheese plant they would fill out a detailed questionnaire about the cheese plant and what their objectives were. One of the questions was what is your greatest obstacle doing business in Russia. Generally they answered corruption but as the years went by that changed to competition. The director would ask me what we can do now. My answer always was you have to make a better product. They seem to think that would be an endless task. I said that it's not impossible to make a better product and those who don't will fail. But this is not going to happen to us. I felt optimistic because most of these new Russian business men and women were young people who weren't encumbered by the old communist cradle-to-grave security. Over the years I spent in Russia I could see many joint ventures that teamed up with European firms in the cheese, beer, wine, dairy and food product industry producing world-class products.

Wednesday, February 19, 1997

I went to the farm with some of my detergent to run through their pipelines. We mixed it and observed how it cleaned the pipelines. Then we went to the cheese factory and packaged all of the blocks of muenster except for some which we did not have bags for. Then we packaged all the curd. We cut some cheddar cheese in consumer size pieces and wrapped in plastic wrap that is sealed on a hot plate. We used up all the bags so we are not making any cheese until we get more supplies.

We returned to the farm and drained the cleaner in the pipeline and added an acid cleaner. We noticed a greater degree of cleanliness in the pipeline however there was still milk stone which we were unable to remove. Milk stone is the residue left on the surface after heating milk. The problem was we could not reach a temperature in the solution to clean the pipeline properly. There were several elements in the hot water heaters that had burned out and they were unable to repair them. For the time being we had to live with that. We overcome that somewhat by utilizing the milk quickly before the bacteria count got exceedingly high.

I returned to the factory and took some packaged milk to instruct Tania on the use of our microscope to do a DMC (direct microscopic count). We diluted the methylene blue with alcohol in water for two minutes. Tonya set up the microscope and we were able to focus on bacteria readily because of the poor quality of the milk. Tonya had worked in a medical laboratory. She and her family later left for Germany as refugees. I was very disappointed to hear that but I can understand that her future would be much better her and her children.

Friday, February 21, 1997

Today we had a meeting with all the staff people at the cheese factory and made all the recommendations known which I felt needed to be addressed in order to produce a top-quality cheese. It was a last chance to review any particular problem they may have. Then we presented a poster of the farm and milk house indicating where all the sanitation problems are.

After that we had a small celebration and a toast with champagne then some cake with coffee. In the afternoon they had a ceremony with members of the church. They had a guitar player with a group of singers and some speeches were made. It was sort of the official turning over of the cheese plant to the village. It was a little emotional for me because my work is now done.

I said farewell to some of the workers then I checked in at the town hall and the secretary called Omsk airport and made reservations for my return flight to Sheremetyevo Airport in Moscow. Then I called Citizens Network in Moscow to pick me up at the airport.

The temperature outside dipped to well below zero Fahrenheit and it was the first night I felt cold in the house. However I went to bed soon. Also I got some troubling news reports about the cheese factory. Customs officials want $23,000 for the butter churn and separator plus 3% of every day the fine is not paid. I have no idea how they will solve this dilemma.

Saturday, February 22, 1997

Today was a rest day. Many village people stopped by just to say goodbye and bring some mail for Bill and Betty Peters. We were supposed to go on a one horse sleigh ride but it was just too cold that morning. We made some last-minute phone calls and Bill went to the banya. We played some cards and talked about old times and what I was going to do now that my project had been completed here in Neudochino. I told her I had been asked if I would return to Russia for several different projects teaching cheese making at universities and helping other cheese plants.

Sunday, February 23, 1997

I got up late because it was so cold in the house. I guess nobody wanted to get up and make a fire. We went to church and then we had dinner at our neighbor's house. I packed my bags and they drove me in a Russian four wheel drive jeep to the airport to catch my 7:30 PM flight to Moscow. They wouldn't let me on the flight because the ticket wasn't made out correctly. All tickets were still hand written. They hadn't installed computers yet. So they booked me on the 9:30 PM flight. Citizens Network office was closed on Sunday so we tried to contacted our country representative Scott Edward's at home. His wife said she did not know how to reach him but she would do the best she could to relay the information that I was on a later flight.

I was scheduled to land at Sheremetyovo Airport. There are three different airports in Moscow. My plane landed in Domodedovo Airport. I had not been informed of this. I arrived at one o'clock in the morning and the airport emptied out very quickly. I was stranded. This time I really had to rely on my Russian and find a way to my apartment in Moscow. In Russia there are many people unemployed who use their personal automobiles as taxis but they are not allowed to park at the airport. I had a dozen taxicab drivers approach me wanting to take me back to Moscow. I felt a panic attack coming upon me but I kept telling myself don't panic. I told them "I had a friend that was going to pick me up and he is late". They all disappeared. Along came someone, asked "can I help you?" My Russian came in handy. I told him I was telephoning my friend but I cannot reach him. I'm stranded here at this airport. He said he would take me to Moscow for $100. I told him I was working for an organization called Citizens Network and they only allowed me $50. I don't have $100 on me and he accepted $50 and agreed to take to Moscow. I couldn't believe how far away he parked his car. The mafia controls who can pick up people at the airport and he wasn't licensed to do that. All the airports in Moscow are far outside the city. It takes two hours to get into the city. Here in the US our highway system crisscrosses over the cities and makes it much easier to travel into major cities. In Russia you have to go through the city and stop at a multitude of red lights and endure terrible traffic jams. I asked my driver why my plane landed in a different airport than scheduled. He said it's not uncommon; probably the airline hadn't paid their fuel bill at the other airport. I took him at his word knowing this was Russia with all its turmoil. I finally arrived at my apartment at 4 AM and I was dead tired but relieved. Many thoughts went through my mind about how vulnerable a foreigner can be traveling by himself. Many of my friends back home said to my wife "aren't you afraid to let your husband leave you for Siberia for long periods of times". I never felt endangered or uncomfortable traveling by myself in Russia.

I worked so hard to learn the language. The Russians really respect you, give you a lot of creditability and extend their friendship when you speak Russian. If you are aware of your surroundings you are as safe as traveling in any big city in the US. We were always warned by CNFA to stay away from nightclubs and bars unless in a group.

Next morning my driver picked me up at the hotel and we went to the Moscow office to be debriefed. Everyone was very excited to interview me and hear about the first cheese factory under CNFA program for American volunteers. I spent the afternoon working on my final report to be submitted to the Washington, DC. I was scheduled the following day on a flight from Moscow to Kennedy International Airport in New York. I was anxious to get home and speak about my accomplishments. Every time my plane lifted off of Russian soil I would look down and say to myself thank God I was born in America.

I have come to know and work with many families while building the cheese plant and training them how to make cheese in their village. Many of these people would tell me about life under Stalin and the purges that followed. We are so blessed our families were born in America.

Mennonite Central Committee

Russia Office of Steve and Cheryl Sherk

It was requested of me to stay an extra two days in Moscow. Several people wanted to meet with me.

Steve and Cheryl Sherk "MCC country representatives" wanted my assessments of my work in Neudochino and in general what some of the obstacles were doing business in Russia.

We had a lengthy discussion about the future of the Neudochino cheese plant financed by MCC. I had to be honest and could not confirm what the future was for this plant. Bill and Betty Peters will remain in Neudochino for another year to oversee the operation and report back any major problems which may incur. I related to him my experiences in St. Petersburg and similar experiences in Neudochino with corruption. I have no idea if we can transcend these problems once we all leave the village. The challenges are different from American-style capitalism.

Imagine starting a business in a land where no credit is offered, no checking accounts, legal cash transactions are rare and barter is the transaction of the day. I know for a fact that some of our cheese production went to oil refineries in Omsk in exchange for gasoline for their tractors. Many workers in the refineries hadn't been paid. They gladly accepted cheese in lieu of payments for back wages.

It is difficult to determine whether they are moving forward making a transformation to a free market economy. I think there are some places where they are doing better.

Democracy usually thrives in the presence of a large middle class, but Russia is characterized by a small number of rich people, and masses of low income workers such as teachers and policemen who haven't always got paid on time.

Land ownership is still a controversial topic affecting private farmers, and nobody is willing to loan money to an agricultural business. There are some private farmers who are making it but I don't know what the percentage is. Other challenges facing Russian cheese makers are low-quality milk and the milk shortage.

There is also the problem of paying for machinery with cash when no credit is available. I tried to promote cheddar cheese curd because it can be made and sold almost immediately. This alleviates a cash flow problem

Credit, Collateral and Private Ownership

As I traveled it always astonished me why the Soviets established a collective farm 100 miles from the city of Omsk and had to transport the milk into the city every day. It certainly had something to do with the Trans-Siberian railroad. When people were exiled into Siberia they were dropped off along the way and that is why they established communities. The railroad does goes by our village of Neudochino.

After our informal get-together and discussion Steve and Cheryl took me out for dinner. He said it was a learning experience for him to talk to somebody that built two cheese plants in Russia. He wanted to give me a tour of Moscow but I said I have further commitments to meet with some Russian business people that wanted to see me before I left. I told him I will be back in Moscow in a few months and I will accept that offer.

Some of My Observations of Business in Moscow

Moscow's Raddison Hotel

I will always remember sitting in my hotel room picking up the Moscow Times, reading about Paul Tatum, the first American businessman murdered in Russia. He was a co-owner of the Radisson Slavyanski Hotel and published a full-page ad addressed to Mayor Luzhkov of Moscow. The article read "come out of the shadows into the bright sunlight, stand up against organized crime and their dangerous activities". He was assassinated shortly afterwards. It portrayed how corrupt Russian business had become and sent shockwaves through the halls of our Congress in Washington DC. Paul Tatum was an American businessman, formerly a Republican fund raiser who was a co-owner with a Russian businessman, Umar Dzhabrailov.

Dzhabrailov, a Chechen, had many political connections in Moscow. Interpol had him listed as a member of a Chechen organized crime unit. The Radisson Slavyanska hotel had a conference center in downtown Moscow. It was a place where Wall Street financiers, Texas oilmen, politicians and other VIPs could rendezvous and conduct their business while staying in Moscow.

I had an appointment with the head chef of the Radisson. He was a Canadian who wanted American-style dairy products, especially mozzarella for pizzas which we were intending to produce in Uglish, Russia. There were many businessmen from across the world that stayed at this hotel and they want to have a very cosmopolitan menu for all their foreign guests. I went there with a Nickoli Shergin who wanted my help to start manufacturing mozzarella for the pizza industry. This Italian-type cheese that has a stretch characteristic is something not available in Moscow. My Russian friend said if he approached the chef on a sales call he wouldn't give me the time of day. You being an American he can relate better as what his needs are.

Ikea Builds Store in Moscow

There was a bribery scandal when Ikea, Swedish furniture giant, opened shop in Russia. It was alleged that they allowed bribes to be paid to a contractor to resolve an electrical supply problem at their store in St. Petersburg. The company said that a Swedish tabloid newspaper wrote the story detailing the bribes. Ikea once publicly stated that it never committed itself to corruption. This news came as a shock to its clean-cut reputation. There were many articles in the news media about their shopping mall businesses in Moscow with city authorities.

Wal-Mart in Russia

I was always somewhat puzzled why there were no Wal-Marts in Moscow or any large city in Russia. It has been rumored that they have made attempts to establish Wal-Marts in Russia but they will not commit themselves to paying bribes. They opened an office in Moscow early on because of their interest in the Russian market. If McDonald's were so successful why couldn't Wal-Mart. I have been surprised by the number of small supermarkets that have established themselves in Russia, very modem, clean and loaded with some of the finest food products in the world.

The first McDonald's Restaurant in Russia:

I remember when the first McDonald's restaurant opened in Moscow. It was the largest McDonald's restaurant in the world. While I was in Moscow I went to a McDonald's restaurant on the Arbat located on Teverskaya Street where most of foreigners go to buy their Russian souvenirs. When it opened, there were long lines around the block. The meal for a family was the cost of one week's salary for the average Russian at that time. Boris Yeltsin was invited for the grand opening. I don't think he was impressed with the Big Mac. He said it needs more salt. Now there are McDonald's in every major city in Russia. Several times when I was traveling in Russia my driver would say "let's grab a bite to eat; you want to go to McDonald's"? No I want to go to a Russian restaurant for some borscht, meat and potatoes. I like the atmosphere and camaraderie with fellow Russians. My driver said "me to". He said McDonalds is for the young crowd who don't know what good food is. I often wondered how McDonald's was so successful in Russia. There were never any reports of any bribes or corruption.

There was an interesting book published by Mr. George Cohen who was the CEO of McDonald's in Canada. They signed an agreement on a joint venture in the city of Moscow. Possibly they were able to make a deal in Moscow and satisfy the authorities with a share of profits. Of course this is only my speculation. They certainly were successful in Russia.

In many restaurants in Moscow there always was a security guard at the door. I asked my translator why they need law enforcement officers at the entrance. She told me they want to keep undesirables out like the Mafia and unscrupulous tax officials and several other reasons she did not wish to discuss.

Indeed this was a major part of our conversation with Steve Sherk and his wife Cheryl exchanging ideas and knowledge about doing business in Russia.

I returned to my hotel and packed my bags for the flight back to the US in the morning.

Future of Neudochino Cheese Plant in Jeopardy

The new director of the village took out a $300,000 loan from the bank for the village to upgrade the dairy barn and infrastructure of the village. He took the money and fled to Germany leaving the village in debt to the tune of $300,000. I found it very difficult to get accurate information and everything was quite murky. I wrote a letter in Russian and sent it to Andrei Einns, former director, who earlier left the village for Germany. I stated this new director should be extradited, brought back and put into prison. I am sure Andrei knows most of the details. I received a notice that it really doesn't concern me and I should be careful about my getting involved and not do any investigating. I do know as a fact that at that time the KGB and Communist Party were still quite strong and in control of the political system and agricultural communities especially in Siberia. When Putin became president he quickly reasserted control of Russia's regions and republics. There are 89 regions in Russia like we have 50 states here in the United States. In the aftermath of the terrorist attacks in Russia, Putin announced plans to restructure Russia's regional and national Governors. He was able to enforce a method himself, selecting governors for the 89 regions in the federation. He justified these changes as necessary to unite the country against terrorism, in affect significantly increasing the power of the Russian president.

When I was on assignment in Podsosnova, a village near Barnaul, I was asked if I could meet with two men who had a milk drying operation. They wanted to know if I had any knowledge about making cheese out of dry milk powder. I have done this consistently with cottage cheese. However, I never tried it on hard cheeses like cheddar or gouda cheese. They mentioned a village near Omsk. They we're taking the milk to a powder plant and drying it. Unfortunately I failed to document their names. They had no idea that I was the American that shipped the cheese plant to the village. I was quite skeptical and I did not render much more information. It was possible they made a connection and asked for no further details and we parted company. I wasn't fully aware what was happening in Neudochino at the time but there was some distressing stories and feedback from Ben Falk. I found it to be very disturbing after all the volunteer relief work we had done. I had another long talk with Ben Falk who keeps in touch with Harry Sawadski in the village. He seems to be one of the very few who has a handle on all ongoing things in Neudochino. Harry has two brothers and one sister but they all moved to Kazakhstan in the mid-1990s but he makes it his business to know as much as possible about these Mennonite villages. He and his wife probably would never move to Germany.

Here the story of Neudochino is a bit mysterious. When Gorbachev, in the 1980s announced Perestroika and Glasnost, he made it possible for every person in the community to become a private citizen, to work his own land if they wish. It allowed any community or village to break from a "Collective Farm" system and become private. Neudochino did just that in January 1, 1992. This was a landmark decision for the village and all documents were successfully filed.

Neudochino broke away from the "Parvomeisk Collective" under the leadership of a man by the name of Rieul. We are not certain about the proper spelling of these names because we are translating them into English by ourselves. Rieul was very unhappy about this because he knew that he would be losing 54% of the total collective farm production of all of the 13 villages that made up the collective farm community. Neudochino had over the last number of years consistently produced dairy and grain products which amounted to 54% of the total collective farm productivity, in other words it was subsidizing the other 12 villages but never getting any more credit from Moscow than 1/13th of the total. When this privatization possibility became a reality Neudochino jumped for it. This made Rieul very uncomfortable. Many Russian communities were not able to meet their quota and always relied on the Neudochino farm to help cover their quotas by subsidizing them.

When Andrei announced that privatization was now a possibility and a reality, Rieul would become the director of the village. Residents put up a fight to prevent him from becoming the new director. They just did not want him and were successful in removing any possibility of him becoming the manager of Neudochino. He knew very well that without Neudochino being in the collective farm system he would be out of a job.

Also, this meant that each man, woman and child over 18 would now be eligible for their share of the total property, which in this case in Neudochino worked out to be 37 hectors of land for each individual. The paperwork finally became available only seven years ago. The group of three families that Ben Faulk supported now farm 600 hectors of land. They just received the paperwork and deeds for this property as of two years ago. Ben strongly urged these families to go private. However they are not farming it all because it is too much for them to handle and some of the land is located in different areas. They rent some back to the owner of the village and he pays them good rent. As the three families grow in number they have plans to farm it all.

In addition all those who in their hearts and minds were set on migrating to Germany, could if they were lifelong residents of Neudochino, claim and deed their property over to remaining families and even friends in Neudochino. Those who did not bother to make this arrangement, lost their share of land and the possibility of never acquiring it again or coming back to settle in Neudochino. This transaction needed to be completed by January 1, 2011; otherwise all the unclaimed property reverted back to the Russian government. Today there is considerable property that once was in Neudochino's village collective farm system owned by the Russian state. Harry says, "It is so sad because if only the people had acted sooner, much of the land could have remained with the residents of the community". Also if those living in Germany did not deed their property to remaining family or friends before 2011, they could never come back to live in the village. It was lost forever.

Now it Becomes a Bit Cloudy

The village went into default at the end of 2006. A Russian man, Martni, became director of the village. He was to have taken out huge bank loans, but never applied them to the village operation. He fled to Germany with the money. They have been looking for him ever since but without success so now this becomes a village debt crisis.

Now it becomes even more obscure. A man named Kuriachikov who had major interest in the Tatarsk Powder Milk Plant paid off the bank loans of 6 million rubles. He took ownership of the village putting his own manager of the village in place. I have a strong suspicion that this is the person that I met in Popsonova on a previous assignment. By this time all of Neudochino's milk was going straight to the Tatarsk plant to be made into dry milk powder. The cheese plant in the village lost their milk supply.

Now Rieul reappeared and went into partnership with Kuriachikov but that business relationship was very short lived. The Tatarsk milk plant operation was declining and was now up for sale.

I found much of the antiquated equipment in the milk plants. Now they have to pay the world fuel prices and no longer are as highly subsidized as they were in former days. It takes huge amounts of capital thus requiring huge amounts of milk in order to be efficient. This is not an option in Russia yet. The Tatarsk Milk Plant was up for sale. Two men from Slavgord purchased the plant and took over the 6 million rubles Neudochino debt. The men Siroff and Samkin were now in control. They were strictly businessmen. They kept the Tatarsk dairy plant but resold the village's debt and its potential to two other men, Machsienoff and Harry, forgot his last name. He appointed a manager named Simonoff who they feel is doing a good job in Neudochino now.

Machsienoff is now the sole owner of the village of Neudochino, and the Tatarsk milk plant. He was amazed at the success and the profitability of the Neudochino dairy and the farm. The ground is so rich and the prospects for the future are great. He already purchased three new large combines, several large tractors and numerous other pieces of equipment and is very optimistic about the future of working there in the village. Harry says the village debt to Machsienoff is very large and the village will perhaps never be returned to the residents. He says no one in the village could take on that kind of responsibility. Simonoff is working well with the village and all seems to be going quite well. The private farmers are able to sell all the products they produce and have their land and it generates rent income. They are part of only 12 Mennonite families remaining in the village and over 100 Russian families. Life has improved. A number of homes now have hot and cold running water, kitchen cupboards, indoor washroom facilities, clothes washers, and a better disposable income than they ever had before.

Machsienoff is also reaching into the village in other ways. A very large new dairy barn is being built. The hog barn that burned down is being totally rebuilt. Ben Falk said it looks very good with all new materials. There may be a new dairy plant in the plans, so I wonder what will happen to the cheese plant that is there now. Of course Andrei Einns owns that and it may continue on its own taking all the milk from individuals who have a few cows. This is good for the village.

Ben said, "Tony, this will probably generate a lot of questions for all of us", yet of course that is good too. When talking to the people the story seems to be a little different each time, we will continue to keep up the dialog and try to keep informed; maybe the story will change.

The last word I receive was good news. Ben informed me that there are individual small family farms shipping milk to our cheese plant and they are making cheese and producing a variety of other products. Harry has purchase delivery vans and is making several trips a week to surrounding villages supplying them with their Neudochino food plant products. They not only make cheese but meat products. We here in America will never realize the difficulties that Russian people had to face in this transition. Although this information may be a bit nebulous I trust it is as accurate as I can recall.

Uglish Russia: Nickoli Shergan
Director of Research Center for Russia

I arrived in Moscow where I met Nickoli Shergan who drove me to Uglish. It is an old town in the Yaroslavl region and belongs to Moscow's golden ring. It's famous for its watchmakers and also for its splendid cheeses and other dairy products. The agricultural scientific research center for all of Russia is located here. Located nearby is a factory where they produce all of their cultures and rennet for cheese making.

Today Uglish being on the Volga River is a stopover for tourists on cruise ships from St. Petersburg to Moscow because of its historic nature. After Ivan the Terrible's death, his son, Prince Dmitry, was sent to Uglish with his mother and was killed here at the age of eight under uncertain circumstances. The Church of Dmitry is one of the famous landmarks of the town built where Dmitry died.

In Uglish a team of restorers have been working on the town's historical center since 1952. Being a member of our landmark society in my community, I can relate to the efforts made trying to save historic landmarks. I spoke to some of the people who are involved in restoration and how they struggle to find the funds when so many people are below the poverty level. I remember traveling by car though Siberia and passing through many small settlements and seeing these massive stone and wood onion-domed churches built centuries ago. Many are falling into ruin. Many were destroyed by Stalin or turned into other uses. I believe there is a renaissance in Russia for old architecture. Even old wooden log house are being restored, but many more are disappearing through neglect and poverty.

I met Nickoli Shergan at the ACDI-VOCA office to discuss my assignment. Nickoli was the director of the Russian Research Institute for Butter and Cheese Making. He had a PhD in dairy science and his wife Irena also had a PhD in dairy microbiology. She was director of the department of microbiology and taught students to become lab technicians in milk, cheese and butter testing. There was a large cheese manufacturing facility at this site; it took up a whole city block. It always appeared to me that in Russia when they built these facilities they boasted they had the largest plant and Research Center in the world.

As the director of the Institute, Nickoli Shergan had not been paid on a regular basis. He had decided to take his career on a new path and become a private consultant for the cheese industry in Russia on a payment basis. He was an expert in Russia type cheeses. He lacked the knowledge for making foreign type cheeses. Our plan was to travel around Russia to different cheese plants that would invite us to take part in this endeavor. I would show them how to make processed cheese, cheese spreads, cheese curd, cheddar, gouda, mozzarella and other varieties. We were mostly welcome but several plants denied us access. They felt they had secrets to preserve... or just show no interest.

He also wanted to have his own research center. We visited the Russian Watch factory which was partially vacated. A Mr. Buckin is part of joint venture manufacturing food processing equipment. They have already built a prototype cheese curd mill required to make cheese curd. Also, they built a device to wrap consumer size cuts of cheese for delis and stores. This machine has been exhibited at the food show in Moscow.

There was a large food canteen and facilities for food preparation at this factory for all its employees. This is very common in any plant with many workers. Everyone got a hot meal at noon. The canteen was no longer needed since most all workers were laid off. Scientific Production Center of Dairy Research, as it was name by Nickoli Shergan, wanted to set up their research facilities here. This would be ideal for a research center. They could also develop their own machinery. They have a machine shop and trained machinists who have been unemployed for many months. They are anxious to pursue making any type of new machine to meet our needs.

We also visited another factory interested in his research facility. The director gave us a tour. They are now manufacturing digital scales, the type used widely in the US in deli food stores. They are now widely accepted in Russia.

I purchased a scale for my personal use as a souvenir. These engineers are anxious to find markets for their scales. They went through the trouble of manufacturing a scale in ounces and pounds for me instead grams in kilograms.

Developing New Cheese Products for the Uglish Market

Nickoli Shergan became the chief production officer of the cheese manufacturing facility. They were making gouda cheese. I reviewed this operation and made several recommendations. In Russia in all hard cheese operations they would put the wheels of gouda cheese on wooden shelves for approximately six weeks. This cheese would become covered with mold, producing lingering off-flavors. The Russians were so used to this cheese, they considered it normal. When the cheese was fully cured it was put onto a washing machine to remove the mold and move to a dryer. Then the cheese would be waxed and boxed. It does not take much mold to completely contaminate the water in this machine, it was an unsanitary operation. I have been in many cheese factories in Russia and this method was utilized in every plant.

I urged Nickoli to stop this procedure. I recommended using a different culture that is use in gouda production in Holland. It produces a characteristic soft mellow flavor that produces small eyes (holes) associated with naturally aged gouda cheese. I had some samples of a food grade material called delvicide to prevent mold growth. After several weeks we vacuum packed the cheese in cryovac bags and cured it at 50° F for another month.

Several months later he came to me and he was very proud because he had won several gold medals for the quality of his cheese. In an exhibition in the city of Krasnodar, they held a cheese judging contest where cheese plants from a wide area entered their products. It is like our New York State Fair.

Our next project was to develop processed cheese spreads. In our US plant we manufacture processed cheese spreads with a multitude of different condiments and flavors such as garlic, hot pepper, dill, horseradish, and etc. I had carried with me many of these flavors, stabilizers, emulsifiers and food coloring. Nickoli turned this project over to his wife Irina and her laboratory staff at the research center.

We also used Russian emulsifiers and stabilizers. We made twenty different samples of cheese spreads using various formulas. We varied the moisture and pH and used different cheese in each batch. We invited about a dozen people involved at the research center and did a taste test. We picked four different formulations and then narrowed it down to one or two that we will use in our commercial production. We are now producing cheese spreads in the Uglish area. To this day I don't know how far their marketing region is. Several years ago I spoke to my coordinator at ACDI-VOCA in Moscow. She told me that it was available in stores where she had been shopping. The clerk told her it was develop by an American. I felt this was a major accomplishment.

It took a lot of time and effort but it was done very professionally and we accomplished our goal. Nickoli said all my life I have been in academics. I hopefully intend to have my own business. Nickoli Shergan and his new company are undergoing the establishment of a seminar training course. We will be able to teach potential cheese makers how to develop new cheese products.

We aim to a start farmers' co-operative and conduct seminars in the various aspects of developing quality milk products, manufacturing of dairy products, food safety and marketing techniques. All members will have to meet all the sanitary regulations and standards similar to the US standards in the cheese industry.

This new company has already conducted seminars with over 40 people in attendance. 10 more are in the planning stage or have been held at this time.

I hope to volunteer my time and participate in the seminars. I feel it would be beneficial if I could assure this cheese was marketed well when a potential customer desires our product

I urged Nickoli to continue with research and development, which we began. We developed a cheese spread production and won several gold medals. It still has a low volume of production but it is growing. I would like to see the production of processed cheese. It's an opportunity to utilize under grade cheese, which sometimes is sold at a lower price. Nickoli apparently was a bit hesitant to make processed cheese with flavors unless he could realize an increase in the overall profitability by using some of his dry whey. Because of the shortage of milk he has a market for all his cheese. Now the biggest obstacle is competition, especially from Moldova, Belarus and Ukraine because of their lower milk prices.

The tourist traffic is increasing yearly in Uglish. There is a vodka museum and watch factory, which attract many people. Uglish is also the center of cheese production and research where cheese cultures and rennet are produced. The present cheese making facility has a viewing galley. In former days it was a show place for Russians to see cheese being produced.

Moscow is providing financial support to build a five million dollar hotel and casino in Uglish. Construction is to begin this year. Many new Russians are buying property to build summer residences on the Volga River.

I am well aware some of my recommendations are a bit ahead of times but everything is changing rapidly in the Russian agricultural sector of their economy.

One of Nickoli Shergan and my basic objectives visiting Russian cheese factories was to introduce ourselves and work alongside cheese makers sharing each other's technology. In the future Nickoli can disseminate this information through his new company. We combined our efforts teaching cheese makers how to develop American-style cheese. We put our emphasis on Italian mozzarella because pizza was becoming a very popular snack in Russia. He commented many times, "Now I am also a volunteer where in previous times I was paid to do this. Hopefully my Scientific Research Center in Uglish will be up and running and I will be able to charge a fee for my services and knowledge".

We visited only two plants that were quite successful in making mozzarella, Lubim and Varakavo. They were located in a rural area north of Moscow. I was surprised when I arrived and saw a prefab cheese plant shipped from a Scandinavian company. This community was created in an area where large natural gas fields exist. There were upwards of 500 to 1000 people working at the location. This was all part of the communist system where they set up self-sustaining communities with a farm, housing, processing food plants and schools.

These were very small prototype dairy processing units built on platforms in sections and shipped on site and assembled. We were very well received in the community. They were very interested in producing cheese from their milk. Our main goal was to try to make mozzarella to sell for the pizza industry to generate a profit for this village

Return to Moscow

Pizza Hut opened their first franchise in Moscow and Nickoli and I made a visit there. It was very expensive but there seemed to be many customers. Much of their cheese was imported from Poland. Moscow does not portray a true representation of Russia. It is one of the most expensive cities in the world. Pizza Hut later closed the restaurant for reasons unknown.

Sean Shinners and his wife Polly were in Moscow at the time. He was from Buffalo and President of the Buffalo-Tver Sister City program. He was visiting Valery Plonkin and his wife Svetlana, President of Trado Bank in Trver. He had many contacts in Russia and was interested in joining our efforts to introduce these new products to hotels, restaurants and food distributors in Moscow.

Nickoli Shergan and in the rest of us drove to Starista. We met with

Nikolai Ushin, director of a very large cheese plant. He was also interested in mozzarella. He had a small experimental vat and he was gave us milk and let us demonstrate the making procedure for mozzarella cheese. He gave us a tour of the plant and introduced me to Ludmilla. She was the lady that was going to help me make this cheese. However, he later informed us that he was not interested unless we were committed to investing money in his plant. The plant already was carrying a heavy debt load. He could not see any profitability in producing this new product unless we produced several tons per day. This always concerned me when talking to Russian cheese plant directors. This was always the mentality of the communist's planned economy where you were told what to produce and there was no need to market what you produced. I tried to explain you need to set up a research and development department and market your products. In my opinion in Russia a market already exists, but you have to start somewhere. I always told them we started out very small in the US and we been in business over 60 years, something you don't accomplished overnight.

That evening we walked around the village of Starista. Nikolai gave us a tour of the city and we visited Ivan the Terrible's residence. This was used on his travels from Moscow to St Petersburg in the 1500s. Ivan the Terrible had the famous St Basil's Cathedral built in Red Square in Moscow as a tribute to God. Nikolai briefed us on the history of the area and said it was held by the Germans during World War II. With a four-wheel drive vehicle we all traveled down to the Volga River on some back roads. It was lovely place, typical Russian scenery with white birch tree forests.

Sunday, August 31

The dairy plant owns its own residence where I stayed. I was picked up by Nikoli and Sean and Polly at the cheese plant along with Valery Plonkin and wife Svetlana. We all went on a picnic along the banks of the Volga River. We had plenty of cognac, wine and beer. They cooked shish-kebabs and various other delicacies. They also had fried some fresh fish caught out of the river.

In my brief conversation with Valery, he informed me that banks aren't generally interested in loans to agricultural because of risk factors and long durations of loans. They preferred short term loans with high interest rates. One of the largest banks in Tver had gone bankrupt, he said they played political games and paid the price. I really never got a clear explanation but I realized there was a financial crisis in Russia.

They had 200 acres of land which they converted into a small dairy and a sporting lodge for hunting and fishing. Next to the lodge was a banya built out of logs where we all took a bath and had massages with birch branches.

We all toasted each other to friendship between America and Russia which again left me slightly tipsy. I discovered they had their own Vodka still. I noticed bags of sugar nearby and didn't believe it when they told me the vodka comes right out of the ground. This makes it a fabulous place to have a picnic. What he meant was the water to dilute the alcohol to 80 proof comes from a natural spring. I asked what they made it out of. He said, "Oh you can make it out of anything that contains sugar". My thoughts turned to the quality of this vodka. I asked Nickoli if this was legal. He said yes, "it's legal if you're someone of status and have the right credentials".

You can make vodka out of potatoes, grains or plain sugar. It's from the grains that it gets its flavor. They got water from a natural spring that is soft with minerals. It's these minerals mixed with the grains that separate Russian vodka from other world brands.

Sean and Polly left and took some mozzarella and cheese curd we made to Moscow to take to the Radisson Hotel. I went home and I was very happy to go to bed and sleep off this homemade vodka.

I always wondered why vodka really doesn't have any flavor. That's because whatever it's made out of it is pure alcohol and the proper alcohol is achieved by just adding water. Therefore they may be right; this vodka comes right out of the ground.

Back to Russia
March 5, 1998 Saturday
I returned to Moscow on yet another assignment and drove to Uglish and met Nickoli Shergan and his wife Irina. She had a wonderful dinner prepared for us and then we returned to Lublin and stayed in a hotel nearby. At the cheese plant we met director, Alexei Anatiljivich. He showed us some improvements he made to the cheese plant and his laboratory. He had provided some equipment for us to make more mozzarella cheese.

He took us to a local restaurant for dinner and we discussed all the financial and political problems connected with this cheese plant. It was a very old plant and needed repairs. As usual the subject always came up about are we ready to invest money in his plant When I informed him as a volunteer I am only bringing my knowledge of cheese making I could feel the enthusiasm evaporate. We thought the director and personnel working with us at the cheese factory realized what our mission really was and were very enthusiastic about working with us.

They provided us with milk which we set with direct vat cultures in their rennet. The cheese turned out very well with proper acid development and proper moisture content. It was made into 5 pound loaves and put in the salt brine for 24 hours. That evening we all went out to dinner again and toasted our success with vodka.

March 8, 1998 Sunday - INTERNATIONAL WOMENS DAY
In Russia International Women's Day is celebrated as a national

holiday commemorating the outstanding merits of Soviet women. After the Second World War, called the Great Patriotic War, there were few men left. Women, to this day, do most of the hard work and struggle to provide for their families. It always amazes me whenever I worked in a cheese plant with women doing all the work. The men would be there if a machine broke down. The men at the cheese plant called themselves engineers and would keep the machines running.

Divorce is so prevalent in Russia. My interpreters were very educated and invariably would be divorced. Much of this high divorce rate was a result of men drinking too much and many times less being educated than their wives. The burden of providing for the family would fall on the women causing stress on marriages.

In the US we celebrate Mother's Day but not with the same profound meanings of our counterparts in other parts of the world.

In the US women working in the textile industry protested the low wages and bad working conditions. They started a movement to change life and struggles for equal rights with men in the late 1800s. Many of these people were immigrants from Eastern Europe. This was somewhat synonymous with International Woman's Day.

Late that afternoon we took a tour of the village and there was another celebration. It was children saying goodbye to winter. They made the most beautiful snowmen, snow forts and snow sculptures. They had colored water and they would spray it onto the snowmen and the sculptures. This form of art was most interesting to look at. I chatted with the children who were so enthusiastic about this celebration. The whole community came out to enjoy the sunny day. Everybody was on the street, little children were in their sleighs all bundled up in their snowsuits, and the women with their fur coats and fur hats all enjoyed the music .They would say goodbye to winter as warm weather melted the snowmen and the sculptures. You can warm up on a cold day when you are a part of these festivities.

March 8, 9 and 10

This was our last three days making more mozzarella, a cheddar cheese and cheddar curd with great success. The director and some of his staff decided we should go out to a restaurant for dinner and say our farewells. There were many toasts with vodka and the dinner was Russian style with fresh baked bread, vegetables and sausage and then soup with the main course. The next day we picked up some samples of cheese and headed back to Uglish. We were invited to a meeting at the Ministry of Agriculture in the city of Yaroslovl, the government center of the Oblast.

The City of Yaroslov

Nerbert Victor from the Institute in Uglish drove us into the city.

He gave us a tour of this ancient city. It had many Old Russian Orthodox churches along the Volga River dating back to the 17th century. It was Russia's second largest city at one time. We met with Anotoly Zarkov, Director of Agriculture Ministry. He was interested in our program. They were mainly interested in helping the producers of milk that often were not paid on time. I had samples of much of the cheese we produce in our plant in the US. Also there were several of his deputies from the ministry and Nickoli and his wife Irena. They were impressed with the different cheese varieties.

We headed back to Uglish; the weather was turning very cold, 0 degrees Fahrenheit and a March snowfall. I stayed at Nickoli's house that night and the next day we headed by car to Borisoglebski where the owners spent $2 million US dollars. They were making Dutch gouda cheese. The director, Bernard Ter Hoeven, owned a portion of it. He didn't know anything about cheese production and didn't appear to be interested in our program. However, he was an interesting man to talk to. He spoke Russian fluently. We asked if we could have a tour the plant, he refused to show us the plant but he did show us his curing rooms which were newly built. I assumed if the US businessman invested two million dollars it had to be for a new plant. Some information was leaked to me but I could not verify if it was true. I was told Bernard Ter Hoeven took a salary well into six figures.

I had a strange feeling about this operation as if it was a place where money was laundered. It seemed economically unjustifiable for the amount of cheese they were making and the amount of cheese they had in the curing room. We were interested again in making mozzarella cheese and he enlightened me on Russian dealings somewhat. He said "if Pizza Hut is buying cheese from Poland: there are ways of not paying excessive custom fees if you know the right people". So would Pizza Hut really care if it was made in Russia? If we made mozzarella here they would not buy from us, so you're wasting my time. There were so many unclear answers. I was surprised several years later when I was asked to volunteer to come back to this plant. They were having many production and quality control problems. Also, Bernard had been fired.

I will discuss that in a later chapter. I also found out why he wouldn't show us his plant. Only the curing room was new. The rest of the plant needed much repair. Where was the two million dollars spent?

We returned to Lubin by car and then to Varakovo. The weather turned very cold -0 F and we had some heavy snow falls.

March 13-14th

We produced more cheese at the Varakovo plant, our results

were very successful. The director provided us with some additional equipment. Today we are installing water and steam lines. This equipment has never been used. They have been very accommodating to help us in this project.

They had a most interesting device for smoking cheese. We used it to smoke mozzarella and cheese curd. It produced smoke from burning wood and then a switch was turned on and electrically absorbed smoke into the cheese within minutes. It was developed by a group of Russian engineers that worked in the submarine industry. It would absorb smoke in case of a fire or a malfunction on the submarine. I don't know if it will ever be a practical application to smoke cheese commercially. In Russia they still smoke cheese in very large smoke rooms where they hang the cheese or place it on racks. The only problem is if it gets too hot the fat melts out of the cheese. In the US we have companies making liquid smoke flavorings and we incorporate this into the cheese. These companies have laboratories and produce flavors with a pleasant aroma for the food industry. Whenever I mentioned that, they rejected it because they feel it was not natural. We want natural cheese without chemicals or preservatives to prevent mold growth. I was alerted by my translator, she said, "Be careful how often you bandy around the word preservative. It really catches the attention of Russian women who speak no English. The word preservative in Russian translated literally means condoms". I picked up my dictionary and look up condom in Russian and it was pronounced exactly like the word preservative.

We had a brief meeting with director Andrei Alexandrovey. He mentioned that when he buys quality milk he has to pay 1350 rubles per liter which equals to $13.50 per hundredweight in the United States. The problem is the average herd yield in Russia is 6000 pounds per year versus 18,000 pounds per year in the US. I am confident this will improve as Russia improves their herds with genetics and better rations and improved feed supplements. We have volunteer farmers and farm nutritionists who set up dietary programs for cattle.

A car arrived and we packed our bags and went back to the hotel. That evening we went to Nickoli's house where Irena made pizza with some of our mozzarella. She used several different recipes with tomato paste, Russian sausage, mushrooms, and onions with different baking temperatures. We wanted to test the cheese on our pizza to determine how the cheese would stretch. Everyone felt that the pizza was delicious and we didn't need to modify our procedure with our mozzarella.

After that Nickoli showed us films and a video he made when he worked in Switzerland sponsored by the Swiss Academy of Technical Science. He also traveled in the US for several months sponsored by the Commerce Department for people from the former Soviet Union. It was a pleasure working with someone who spoke English so well and had traveled in the US before the collapse of communism.

March 18, 1998

We hired a car to take us to Tver. Then we met with Valery Plonkin and Vladimir Laso, head of the investment and Foreign Economic Relations Department. We had a discussion about the cheese plant at Starista and what we plan to do about our cheese production in the region. We told him Starista was too large for small-scale production. We would start production in another plant and inquired about loans. I told him of my work and what I had done in Russia. They said to me that they would not be interested in the dairy industry in the Tver Oblast due to its low profitability. They turned their attention to the company from Belgium that was investing money into beef production because of higher profit potential. I didn't believe it because of the weather conditions in northern Russia. Southern Russia would be more suitable for beef production where the climate was warmer and cattle can graze on its pastures. At times it can get very depressing when nothing seems to gets approved or accomplished. We all agreed that we would explore other options. Valery Plunkin said "nobody wants to invest in a firm that is losing money". My idea is it will need some kind of government intervention similar to US subsidies that provide funding when farmers are in financial difficulties.

That evening Svetlana and Maria from the housing foundation in Tver met us at the hotel and we went out to a restaurant and had dinner. I wanted to pay but she insisted she would pay for dinner in return for my hosting her for dinner at my house in America and taking her to see a factory where they made prefab housing. After dinner we looked at a housing project that she was involved in. They were row town houses, beautifully landscaped, so typical of suburban America. A Canadian firm had started building a year ago and had yet not been completed. I don't know if it is the Russian system or lack of money but she wasn't happy with her contractors. I have many thoughts about this project from my own dealings trying to complete a project in Russia. We went back to our hotel and had some wine and good conversation and said farewell to one another.

Att: Mr. A. Kutter, J. Price, S. Shinners

SCIENTIFIC-PRODUCTION CENTRE OF DAIRY INDUSTRY

Dear gentlemen!

As I've already informed CNFA in Moscow and Mr. Shinners when he telephoned me we had finished working out all the necessary documentation for mozzarella and cheese curd which were approved by authorities and now production of cheeses is allowed all over Russia. We are able to start production of them in industrial scale at any dairy, sell them and we have an exclusive right for these technologies (set of documentation and copy of sanitary certificate which we will be giving to our customers are valid only when having original seal of our firm and my signature). I congratulate Tony Kutter with our mutual success, his efforts being not in vain, and I'm looking forward for his coming in September. I aggreed with the head of production at Kurganinsk dairy (situated not far from Sochi) that we would come in September to make cheese there. We should meet whith Radisson in Sochi to let them try it and discuss terms of business relations. In addition this man is the owner of one more facility in Adler where some profitable investment may be done and that could be a very good business because of favourable position.

Now we need may be the last step: to make some contracts between all participants of our mutual project, start producing and selling our products. I'm also looking forward for Sean coming here to promote this step. For the last two months I visited many dairies in Russia (situated in Jaroslavl, Moscow, Nowgorod, Tver, Pscov regions) trying to select the one to start with. In some places milk quality in poor, some of them are not interested in new kinds of cheese or located rather far from Moscow or St. Petersburg. They differs in age and quality of equipment, qualification of staff, capacity and many other factors. I found several more dairies where we may start and expand our business. The main problem for majority of them will be stretcher. Soon we'll make a special knife for cheese curd production. As for Sean's tel. call and idea to present our cheeses to Presidents of USA and Russia I totaly support it and I promise any kind of assistance I will be able to do. We may make some cheese together with Tony in Kurganinsk or make it in Lyubim or in Varakovo or in other places. Excuse me please for some delay in sending this fax, I went away to spend a couple of days at a very interesting cheesemaking plant located only approx. 100 km from Moscow which will be of our interest in mozzarella and cheese curd projects. Please let me know by fax about your considerations. I'm looking forward for your reply to start planning more precisely.

Sincerely yours
Director
Fax (08532)-52812
Uglich, 03.08. 1998

N. Shergin

79

Russia's Financial Crisis and Default 1998

When I returned to Russia in 1998 there was a new currency. I remember 5000 rubles to the dollar now it was five rubles to the dollar and inflating quickly. They just removed three zeros. I don't know if I quite understand economic logic and try to makes sense of it. I do know that a devalued ruble makes it much harder to import dairy products from Europe. My argument was when the ruble collapsed in 1998 it was imperative that Russian cheese producers learn to manufacture a broader line of dairy products. It became even more expensive to import cheese.

There are far more dollars than rubles in circulation in Russia. But whenever I went to the shop's to buy food they were not allowed to accept dollars only rubles. I knew there was a formula to determine the price for everyday necessities. On my next trip to Russia the ruble has inflated again from five rubles to 30 rubles to the dollar. I remember talking to a shop owner and he told me I don't have to reduce prices to have a sale, I just leave the price set in rubles and because of inflation people realize it will cost them less.

Ruble Crisis

On May 12, 1998 coal miners went on strike over unpaid wages. Then the railroad workers blocked the Trans-Siberian Railroad. Then there was a run on the bank. People wanted to start selling their rubles and converting them to dollars and nobody trusted the banks. They put their money under their mattresses. I remember pictures in my history books when the stock market crashed in the US and there was a run on the banks. People were actually standing in front of bank shouting and screaming, outraged at what was going on. I witnessed this in Moscow.

The international monetary fund made loans to prop up the ruble. It was later revealed that about 5 billion dollars of these funds were actually stolen when the funds arrived in Russia.

I know this for a fact, our organization ACDI-VOCA in Moscow lost over $1 million of our funds that were in a Russian bank. I asked my US representative in charge of our office in Moscow why the money was in a Russian bank. He told me that was part of the agreement where all funds had to be deposited in Russian banks.

Many Russians I spoke to about the crisis said they would never trust the banks with their savings again. I have often been asked to speak to local organization in my community. I would tell about the desperation of ordinary Russian. What if our US banks failed and all our savings evaporated over night. Then our social security ceased to exist because our government defaulted. Most people react with blank faces and thinking this only happens in foreign countries, never in the US. I try not to let politics creep into my speaking engagements. However, This could happen hear in the US if we don't keep our financial house in order.

Cities in the former Soviet Union where I have had assignment for Citizens Network for foreign Affairs and ACDI-VOCA (Volunteers overseas commerce assignment)

1) Saint Petersburg
2) Moscow
3) Omks
4) Novisibirsk
5) Samara
6) Trud
7) Sochi and Adler
8) Krasnodar
9) Cheressek
10) Novgorod
11) Alti Republic Barrnaul
12) Rostov
13) Uglish
14) Yaroslov
15) Tver
16) Mary-El Republic
17) Perm
18) Vologda
19) Georgia
20) Ukraine Kiev and Lviv

Anatomy of Russian Farms and the Dairy Industry

I can't help assessing Russia's new agricultural economy. After five years and thirteen trips with several more pending, there seem to be a small glitter of hope. Most businessman and tourists traveling to Russia go to St. Petersburg and on to Moscow. Moscow is a cosmopolitan city which does not represent or portray real Russia. Ninety percent of federal revenue collected ends up in Mayor Litzkov's Moscow coffers. He has transformed this one-time drab, austere capital of communism into a vibrant, glitzy, costly high-priced city. Consequently he is so popular he won the last election by 90% of the popular vote. That gives a politician enormous credibility to accomplish his vision of a city to behold by foreigners. There is construction equipment building new hotels, condominiums and office buildings everywhere.

As an American I have a difficult time when one of their Members of the Duma was assassinated and Mayor Luzkov's deputy mayor had an assassination attempt on his life leaving him seriously injured. These crimes are never solved or heard about afterwards. Could we Americans accept these unsolved assassinations if it were a member congress or the deputy mayor of New York? This is not to taking into account all the bankers, businessmen and journalists murdered or that just plain vanished.

After my briefing in Moscow I headed for the hinterland of this huge country to the collective farms and the dairy processing plants. I carry twenty varieties of cheese and dairy products with me. Their centers of dairy research are no longer deseminating information because of lack of financing. Soviet agriculture was the most highly subsidized sector of their economy under communism. Failure to continue this funding was major reason for the collapse of communism. The food wasn't getting on the grocery shelves in 1988.

Most farms and dairy possessing plants have been privatized. They are eagerly looking for new products to broaden their product lines that would increase their profitability. The Russians have a vast array of consumer goods to choose from although much of their cheese is imported. We need to recapture these markets, provide jobs for middle class so they have the money to spend on consumer goods Consumer spending drives the economy in a free market sequence. After Mikhail Gorbachov came many farms were privatized. 8000 collective farms opted to remain as collective farms and the other half became joint stock companies. However, their operating methods never changed.

The quality of milk is inconsistent, the yields are poor and proper feeds and supplements are not available in their feeding programs. Many animals have high sesmetic cell counts. Hardly what a cheesemaker wants to hear as he attempts turn his cheese into a world class food product.

Lake Selizharovo

A car arrived from Selizharovo which is about 100 miles from the city of Tver. We drove to Selizharovo arriving at the administration office and met with a director of the regional government. We discussed our plans and objectives and met with the directors of a milk processing plant nearby. Our driver, Sergei Rozmaitov, took us to the dairy and we met the farm director Sergei Patrovich. We went to the dairy and toured the faciliy. It was a plant where milk from local farms was transported to the city. It only had equipment to cool and pasteurize milk. Then it was shipped in cans or tank trucks to the market place where people would come with their own containers to buy milk. Mayor Lizkov of Moscow passed a law that prohibited milk from being sold unless packaged.

They were interested in looking for investors to buy modern bottling and packaging equipment and to make cheese. They had absolutely no money to build a new facility. The building was very small and substandard. The director had already informed us that it would be unprofitable. After speaking to him and the director of the farm I could not assure him that there would be any investments coming from the United States for a joint venture

At 6 PM they took Nickoli Shergan and me to our apartment. Sergei Patrovish came back with 3 bottles of vodka, a bottle of cognac, bread and sausage. He also brought along Michail, a friend from the bank. They stayed up until 11:30 PM and consumed two liters of vodka and cognac I think I learned how to cope in this situation. I would just take a small sip, set my glass down and so on the next round when they went to fill my glass there wasn't much room for more vodka. Wherever we went they would wine and dine us. They all had an immense ability to consume vodka. They would get into some interesting discussions on everything from cheese making to politics and Russia. When they were conversing in Russian and drinking and joking I was kind of out of the conversation. Nickoli was an excellent interpreter and fluent in English. He was so engrossed in his arguments he didn't have time to translate very much. They were always asking me to tell a joke or anecdote from America and the more obscene they were the more Nickoli and his friends drank and the louder they laughed. Of course that called for another toast. I finally excused myself and went to bed after I took a couple aspirins so I could sleep.

Drinking has been a social problem in Russia even in historic times. I found that I don't have a problem with drinking two or three glasses of vodka because it's usually with dinner, and that lasts 2 to 3 hours with many food courses. I always remember reading in the Moscow Times whenever there was a cold spell they would report homeless people dying on the streets of Moscow at night. They would become drunk and fall asleep on the street and suffer from hypothermia. I remember they would always give me a gift to take back to America and it was usually a bottle of vodka. At one time I could buy a six-pack of vodka on the street in the kiosks like you would buy a six pack of coca-cola. I cannot imagine drinking vodka from a 12 ounce aluminum can. I would carry this vodka back home as a souvenir. Selling this vodka in aluminum cans was abolished very early on. Much of it was unregulated. There has always been alcohol abuse in Russia. The government has tried to reduce alcoholism by education. Mikhail Gorbachov also tried this without success.

Whenever we had dinner they said we only drink like this when we host our American friends. I think they were only joking. These toasts can be cordial and heart warming. The next morning Sergei and Mikhail arrived at our flat at 10 AM and they had two bottles of vodka with them. Again we had several toasts with lunch in the restaurant.

Then we went to the forest where there was a spring of water which was just above freezing it was a sunny day maybe around 25°. There was like a small park in its middle of a forest where there were several buildings, one of which was a chapel where you could pray for health and prosperity. There was a small spring with crystal-clear water constantly overflowing about 5 foot deep. There was a religious belief that if you plunged into the water over your head three times it would cure all of your minor ailments. You would feel very comfortable, refreshed and invigorated. Nickoli was the first one to strip down to his underwear and plunge into the waters three times. To my amazement he seemed to suffer no ill effects. I assume this water was probably around 45°F because water constantly flowing from underground usually has a higher temperature than the surrounding air. They urged me to join them in this ritual. I rolled up my pant legs and submerged my feet up to my knees, it didn't feel all that cold but I wasn't about to jump in over my head. They said to me, "You're a religious man that goes to church, join us in this customary tradition". I said, "I don't feel that I'm quite that religious".

Mikhail, our driver, was so drunk he stumbled in the snow and we convinced him to return to the car and sleep. I was worried about the situation but everybody told me not to worry he's known very well and has connections. We returned to the car and woke up Mikhail and headed for Lake Selizharovo. He appeared to have sobered up somewhat but we stopped three times along the way to have a toast of vodka.

There was a collective farm of several thousand acres which stretched along the shores of the lake. It was a beautiful area with birch tree forests so symbolic of Russia. The director of the collective farm had a vision of building a hotel and a resort complex for Russian oligarchs to hunt the forests for elk, moose and wild pigs.

I just couldn't comprehend exactly what was going on. I was under the impression they wanted to show me their collective farm. They showed me an interesting project they were working on, composting cow manure with worms. They told me this project was developed at a university in California. They even imported the worms from California. When it was completely composted it was packaged in plastic bags and used it for gardens in dachas.

We returned to the hotel, Sergei was driving erratically and at a high rate of speed. I was concerned for our safety. As we entered the village a policeman flagged us down at a routine checkpoint. I thought for a moment we were in some serious trouble. Mikhail was in the rear seat so drunk he could not walk and our drivers had at least a pint of vodka in him. Our driver grabbed all his credentials and departed from our vehicle to approach the policeman. He flashed his credentials in front of the policeman and he recognizes him as one of the village officials immediately. He called him by his first name and told him to continue on.

I asked him how come we were not fined because we weren't even wearing seatbelts which almost always commands a fine. Nobody wears a seat belt unless they are approaching a checkpoint at which point ever one buckles up. He said, "You know this is

Russia, it's who you know and who you are". We got back to our flat at 6 PM went to a restaurant for supper then we went back to our hotel and watched some television. I always liked to watch the Russian news especially the international news about Washington DC. We were tired and we went to bed at 9 PM. At 1:30 AM Sergei, our driver, was to pick us up and take us to the station to catch the train at 2AM out of Selizharvo. He failed to show up. We missed the train. All we could do was go back to bed and wait til morning to make a decision.

Monday, March 22

Nickoli Shergan went to the town hall to inquire about Sergei's failure to pick us up. They tried to reach him by telephone and they said he wasn't there. There were some conflicting reports that he had a problem with the car and also overslept and was highly possible that he was drunk. My impression was that he was unhappy abot not finding investors for hotel project and cheese plant. Nickoli went to the town hall and found someone who agreed to drive us to Tver for $100. This was half the distance to Moscow. CNFA sent a car to the Tver railroad station where they picked me up and drove me to Komenta hotel in Moscow. The following morning at the CNFA off there was a message for me from Amberg Food Distributing. They had heard of my work in Russia and our cheese plant in Neudochino. They were interested in American-style cheese like cheddar and mozzarella. I left them with a sample of mozzarella that we had produced in several plants with Nickoli and turned it over to him and told him to follow it up. They said they would give it to their customers and check to see if they were satisfied with the product. They would be very interested in distributing cheese if the quality was consistent. They claimed they had 75 restaurants and hotels that they were food servicing.

I called Steve Sherk, MCC Country Representative, because we were getting some distressful feed back from Neudochino. He and his wife Cheryl met me at a metro station in downtown Moscow. We went to a Russian fast food restaurant and discussed the problems at the cheese factory in Neudochino. I felt that the director of the village was undermining our operation. They really need to make some tough decisions about its future. There really wasn't much I could do at this time. I felt my work had been completed. MCC had Bill and Betty Peters overseeing the cheese operation for another year. I never felt that they were included in the decision-making as to the future operation of the cheese plant. We left the restaurant and completed our discussion early because Cheryl and Steve were leaving for Switzerland early in the morning.

In the morning I returned to CNFA for a debriefing. They brought up some questions of concern about on the cheese industry in Russia. If we gave them that technology are they adapting and

utilizing this information. CNFA sent in annual reports to
Washington. This is essential to receive further funding from Aid for
International Development, the chief dispensary of foreign aid in our
State department.

I discussed with them a project that was very successful in Russia
that gave me an idea how we could start an association of cheese
manufacturers. This came about because there was some
volunteers from the mushroom industry who started a Mushroom
Growers Association in Russia. They had seminars on new
technology, marketing, and discussion of all aspects of the
mushroom industry. I met one of the Russians and he said it was so
interesting that he couldn't wait until next year for the next seminar.
He said we had a two day seminar where I met many of my fellow
Russian buyers. This was followed by a dinner, a very enjoyable get-
together.

My first experience picking mushrooms was with Nickoli and his
son Sasha. He showed me which mushrooms were poisonous and
mushrooms that were safe to eat. We started picking and I came
back with a whole basket full of mushrooms. I felt so proud. Nickoli
started picking through them, this one's no good, that one's no good,
when he got all done I only had half a dozen mushrooms. I'm just
glad that I didn't eat any of them while I was picking them, "you
could've been seriously ill", Nickoli said, "Maybe you should enroll in
our mushroom Seminars and learn the basic of a safe mushroom.

This renewed my idea about starting a cheese makers
Association in Russia.

Wednesday, March 24

I flew home and arrived in Washington D.C. on Thursday then took a taxi to the CNFA office and met with Bill Whiting, Russia representative. We had a long discussion about where CNFA could have a lasting impact, he replied that they were happy with my work and would I continue to return to Russia. I told him I would be available again.

The Area and Regions of Karachay-Cherkessia

I have been asked to return to Russia to accept another assignment near Cherkessia. This is a region located in South Eastern Russia. In 1943 the Karachay people were deported to Central Asia for allegedly collaborating with the Nazis. They were allowed back in 1957. It gained republic status in the early 1990s following the collapse of the Soviet Union.

After meeting with Irena Paisova and Helena Savinova, deputy project coordinator, for details of my assignment I flew to Mineral Vodi with my interpreter. We were picked up by Jumbot Khapsirokov President of Saturn Dairy and by his driver and bodyguard. We drove two hours to his residence in Cherkessk. This area of Russia reminded me of the agricultural area of Central California. The weather was warm and it had a very rich deep, black soil.

Jumbot did not speak a word of English and my Russian was not that good yet. I was glad I traveled with an interpreter, but he returned to Moscow the next day. He was only along to check out the project and meet the people requesting my assistance. I couldn't understand why on the way to Jumbot's house he was looking for a place to have a picnic. He had this brand-new BMW automobile. When he found a grassy meadow off the highway with some shade

trees he pulled the car off the road, opened his trunk and there was a roasted chicken and a complete dinner with vodka and cognac. We spread a blanket on the ground and first thing he offered a toast to our friendship and his dream of anew

enterprise. This always seemed to be a natural Russian tradition to go off into the woods some where and have a picnic. I remember many Russian expressions of freedom meant going into the woods.

Under communism people always seemed very reserved in public but more open in private. Our driver never touched any alcohol. Any one in Russia who is a director or person of status always has a driver and is very strict about his driving habits when it comes to alcohol. I always thought Muslims don't drink but there are many Muslims in the world and this is Russia.

After a flight from Buffalo to New York to Moscow and from Moscow to Mineral Vodi I suffered from jet lag. I was still on a high, but vodka can do you in. When we arrived at his home and met his family they had several more toasts and some more to eat. I was ready for a good night's sleep.

Jumbot was a very interesting gentleman and I was well received by his family. He was Muslim; his wife would never eat with us. This is very traditional in their Muslim community. He pleaded with his wife to sit down with us because we were having such a lovely conversation with his friends and neighbors but she said, "no that's for you men but I will have breakfast with you in the morning". I learned that he was somewhat of an oligarch or a new Russian. Under communism he was Minister of Roads and Transportation in this Oblast. Somehow he acquired road building equipment and a cement plant to produce concrete and building materials for highways. I assume this came about when they privatized industry.

With this equipment he built a dairy plant and had purchased all new equipment from Israel. It was a privately owned family enterprise. I visited the plant briefly two years ago and advised them on setting up cheese operation and equipment. They were making sour cream, kefir, Rjazenka (4% fat), Aizan(2.5% fat) (cultured dairy drinks). Also, he had a water bottling operation with state of the art equipment and produced his own plastic bottles. This area has large reserves of mineral waters like, Marzan a medicinal mineral water. These fluid products were the bulk of his operation. What he wanted to do was make cheese with his new equipment. What he also wanted to do was make ice cream. Apparently he had invested some money for ice cream equipment but because of the devaluation of the ruble the ice cream equipment reserve fund had been depleted. Now he had a renewed interest in cheese production. Imported cheeses were increasingly more expensive with payment in dollars. One can imagine it would bolster his domestic production.

He actually started his own bank and named himself president. Nickoli Shergan told me many oligarchs were involved in banking circles to secure funds for their massive operations. Jumbot also showed me a former collective farm that he had an interest in. I assume he had a financial interest in it but I never really got a clear picture and I did not want to delve too deeply in his personal affairs.

There were some tributaries of water connected to the nearby river where one time there were some electric generating facilities. He had dreams of rebuilding all these facilities and establishing a self-sufficient agricultural community. He told me his goal was to be the absolute owner and authority over agriculture in his oblast. He wanted to own the farms that produce his milk and process it into dairy products for the oblast.

Jumbot met us at his bank where he informed us about his long-range plans for his company. It consisted of a farm of 4000 cows with state of art milking machinery at a cost of $3 million dollars. He wanted to acquire huge tracts of land. He is presently trying to acquire a loan from the European Construction Bank, a bank of last resort equivalent to our World Bank in the US. If he could develop this farm he feels he could control the price of milk and set the price of finished products and become profitable. He had some unrealistic lofty ideas and dreams. But his enthusiasm and energy inspired me to work with him and share how I developed my own cheese plant in America.

He would like more volunteers from Citizens Network who are specialists in milk production, animal husbandry, grain and nutrient experts, etc or anything to do with milk production on a large dairy farm. Money appeared not to be a problem for him. I also informed him because of his inability to speak English he should contact Russian Agricultural universities about Organizations that have programs where they take a groups of Russians on tours of American farms. This has been set up by the US Commerce Department in the past I told him.

He employs upward of 100 people in his many operations. I spoke to many of his employees, they were all paid on time, an asset to good employee relations. We trained several cheese makers on his staff to make cheddar cheese, cheddar cheese curd and mozzarella over a three day production run. We also set up a machine to make processed cheese and cheese spreads. They requested that we return on our next trip in the spring when I would be working in the area around Krasnodar. I feel this new family owned enterprise may have a bright future. They were quite happy with the products we produced. I felt it had some off flavors. I could detect farm odors in the product possibly from unclean barns lacking ventilation. We made cheese for several days and I observed all their operations and would like to continue but they insisted that I spend time with their family because it was a Muslim holiday.

Jumbot had a son, Alexander, whom he was very proud of and was grooming to be the director of his operations. I did not actually make cheese with him because they had a director of cheese production, a lady who was very competent and seriously interested about learning how to produce American-style cheese. He also had a cousin Marina whom I met that was an English teacher at the University, who at times helped me with my Russian.

Today was a Muslim holiday where they sacrifice a lamb and distribute to all the families. Then they have dinner and all parents would visit the graves of their relatives. I was invited to participate in this family festivity. I have a great respect for the Muslim people. They are very family orientated and respectful to other cultures. They certainly are not the fundamentalist whom we refer to as terrorists.

It was Sunday, April 28. Alexander, Marina, and I along with Adiek our driver went to the Caucasus Mountains, about a two-hour drive from Cherkessk. They were as beautiful as the Alps in Switzerland with snow-covered peaks year-round. We went to an area called Dombia. It was a winter resort with many hotels for skiers. The hotels were all empty because most Russians after the collapse of communism could not afford to take these vacations. I was informed that because of the war in Chechnya on the other side of the mountains people also were afraid to come here. There was a huge Russian artillery gun in the side of the mountain. Adiek, our driver, said this is our last line of defense. I asked him why are we here if there is a war nearby and nobody else is here. He jokingly said because he doesn't like crowds. Just joking, they fire the cannon to create snow avalanches to protect skiers from this danger. They had a ski lift there and we finally found the operator in the village. He actually came up and turned the ski lift on and we rode to the top of the mountains. it was still covered with snow,very windy and cold. It reminded me of "Zermatt" in the Swiss Alps. We then took a ride down the mountain and we hiked into the woods and had a picnic.

We returned back late that evening and had dinner at Jumbot's House. I was quite tired just from trying to converse in Russian. Of course, at our picnic Marina was with us. I could use her as my interpreter or she would help me with my Russian but at that dinner that evening she was not with us. It is quite stressful when you're trying to express yourself in a limited Russian vocabulary and the other guests speak no English. I could make out with my Russian dictionairy when I was lost for a word. I would always apologize and they encouraged me when they said your Russian is understandable.

Marina arrived later that evening and asked me if I would be able to come to her University and give a lecture to her students about my work in Russia. Jumbot said, "Marina, yes you can have him for a few days but I will need him for cheese making". We all retired for the evening.

The next morning a driver picked me up and took me to the University where I met Marina and several professors who taught English. They were so fluent in English and yet none had ever spent any time in an English speaking country. I gave several lectures about my work. I would introduce myself in Russian and talk a little bit about my family in Russian and I would ask Marina to help me describe the work that we have done in Russia, including a our operation in St Petersburg. Many of the students were reluctant to ask questions in English and would have their professors interpret them for them. I just think they were afraid of making many mistakes and becoming embarrassed. I really urged them to try to speak in English I will understand and I also understand if they make a mistake. I also make many mistakes when I speak Russian but somehow people seem to understand me. So they did open up

90

somewhat and this was very interesting to me and I think as the day went on people got more relaxed and we had a lot of open discussions. I was asked to return several times and speak to different classes. I think Jumbot was getting a little concerned about what my mission was in Cherkessk. The next morning I flew to St Petersburg. My wife Trudy was going to met me there. It was her first trip to join me in Russia.

Jumbot's Cheese Plant in Cherkessia

Sheep in the Caucuses mountains on the road

Artillery used to create noise to create avalanches thus protect skiers

Site of 2014 Winter Olympics

Dombia: Caucasus Mountains snow cover in may

Summit of mountain where skiers will will compete in the

2014 Winter Olympics

Lift to go up the mountain

Jumbot, His Driver, Body Guard and My Translator

Faculty at Language Institute where I was invited

Students studying English where I was invited

Chechnya & Chechen War and Terrorism

I harbored a few concerns about this area of Russia. This area of the Caucasus has been a hotbed of terrorism and wars. Was it safe to volunteer when one hears about businessmen abducted and held for ransom? The Washington DC office assured me this situation was carefully monitored daily and they would never expose Americans if there were the slightest concern. We work in Agricultural areas, terrorist generally target prominent businessmen.

History of Chechen People and Ingushetia

Just another part of their brutal history: Josef Stalin deported whole populations during World War II. They were accused of collaborating with Nazis. More than a half million Chechen people were herded into box cars in the harsh winters and dumped off into no mans land in the snows of Siberia. Most perished from the cold and starvation. Many were never even buried. Many were sent to the Gulags. Historians come to no conclusion on how many perished. Whole families were broken up and children never met up with their parents again.

When Nikita Khrushchev was premiere he condemned Stalin's actions, there was reconsideration from the consequences and Chechens were allowed to return in 1957. Chechens took this opportunity to return to their home lands by the tens of thousands. The majority found their homesteads taken over by ethnic Russians.

This created ethnic tensions and started a separatist movement. The Chechen returnees declared "Rightful Sovereignty" Russia never had intention to honor their independence.
This provoked the first Boris Yelsin's Chechen war with Russian troops.

Beslan School Hostage Crisis:

There were 334 hostages killed, 186 were children. Islamic separatists, mostly Ingush and Chechens demanded withdrawal of Russian troops and independence for Chechnya.

This happed on the first day of school, which is memorable for children and their parents as children sport their new clothes and all the girls have flowers in their hair. Many parents attend school with their child the first day. I recall there were mostly women working with me in the cheese plants and they would take the day off and proudly show me pictures from school the following day.

Nord-Oast Theater Hostage Crisis

The Russian pumped a poisonous gas into a building, no negotiations. Over 170 people died. Again they demanded unconditional Russia withdrawal from Chechnya. There were many more bombings and attacks in the metro systems and apartments, killing and wounding many people.

I can't imagine if one of our states wanted to break away from the United States. Of course we fought a civil war in our history with the greatest casualties in history just to save the union.

There were so many atrocious human rights violations, never any negotiation. Putin vowed to the terrorist "scum" to be taken to the out house and whip them into oblivion.

Novy Edem Cheese Factory
Samara Russia on the Volga

(Novy Edem in Russian means New Paradise from the biblical story of Adam and Eve in the Garden of Eden), Sure is a clever name for a cheese factory!

Samara is one of the larger cities in Russia located in the southeastern part of European Russia. The Volga River has served as a main commercial thoroughfare for Russia for the past several centuries. It also serves as a favorite recreational destination for local citizens and tourists. Samara has very cold winters but hot summers, its beaches are a favorite attraction. I also found it interesting to walk along the streets which boast many old wooden houses and large, beautiful parks in the.

Stalin's Bunker

I have mentioned Stalin's bunker in an earlier chapter. As the Germans almost reached Moscow in 1941; it was to be a reserve Russian capital mainly because of its location. While many of the top Kremlin officials were relocating to Samara, work had begun on the construction of Stalin's bunker. A team of more than 500 building contractors from Moscow, sworn to complete secrecy, were brought to Samara to construct this bunker. An 8 meter diameter shaft down to the bunker was dug by hand to an incredible depth of 37 meters. The project was carried out in complete secrecy. Not even the neighbors knew construction was going on.

Me standing between statues of
Lenin and Stalin

Stalin's command headquarters in case of nuclear attack.

Me with black telephone in event of nuclear attack

This site is now a museum. In the bunker there was a conference hall, offices for top Kremlin brass, living quarters and a dining room. My guide told me that I was considered a very special person and would be taken down the shaft. When I was in the bunker I saw the black telephone to be used in case of a nuclear attack. During the Cold War the Soviet leader could telephone our US president.

Stalin never used the bunker himself. My guide asked me to sit at the desk and hold the phone to my ear so they could take a photo. It seemed kind of hilarious at the time but my memories of the Cold War sent chills through me as I thought of the consequences if Stalin ever had to use this telephone. The Russian guide, an elderly gentleman, spoke fluent German. He told me Franklin Roosevelt had a bunker in the Rocky Mountains of Colorado. I said, "I was never aware of that" but that was actually true!

Novy Edem Cheese Co

Novy Edam cheese plant produces processed hard cheese. I met with Grison Vyacheslav, General Director and Rimma Grishina. Mr. Vyacheslav is a new Russian entrepreneur who has other unrelated business ventures including a furniture manufacturing facility. He was selected and honored as one of the ten most successful entrepreneurs in the Samara Oblast.

His goal was to develop this cheese plant into a modern and highly efficient production facility. Their business plan was to broaden their product line with new varieties and packaging concepts to attract new customers.

Russian people are very traditionally minded consumers with limited incomes. Marketing of new dairy products is very interesting to Russians because of the recent introductions of foreign products. Promotion through advertisement is a part of today's Russia. New Russian businesses must keep in mind they have to answer the demands of the customer.

The majority of cheese manufactured at this plant is processed cheese of excellent quality. The equipment used is very old, however, well maintained. Recently they purchased some German cheese equipment from a closed cheese plant. It was specifically designed for a startup cheese operation and very suitable for hard cheese but it has limited capacity. The overall goals are to develop new types of cheese varieties and experiment with new types of stabilizers, emulsifiers, cultures and flavorings. These are all ingredients I carried with me from the US along with many different varieties of cheese. We want to improve the quality and extend shelf life of finished cheese products. To accomplish this we need to turn their attention to milk quality. This is one of my primary concerns. This is part of our long-range goal and results will be a company with a high reputation and high profits. These are my goals and objectives in my final report to Washington DC.

Rimma Grishina invited her fellow workers to my presentation of numerous cheese samples from the US. It was decided to make cheddar cheese and cheddar cheese curd. We had an excellent milk supply and we started making cheese in the new equipment and produced a very good cheddar cheese. Cheddar cheese has to be aged several months before it can be packaged and sold, however, cheddar cheese curds can be sold immediately as a snack item ,which they were very interested in pursuing. I brought with me packaging materials, cryovac bags to package the cheese in 200 gram packages. Everyone seemed to be excited about the results and felt it was a product that they could easily produce.

Rimma asked me how we should introduce this new product to the market. I said, "if we could go down to City Hall or any government building or office building where there was a large number of people working and set up a table, even if we must pay small fee and give out samples". The next day she told me that we could come down to city hall at lunchtime if we brought a table. We could give out samples of cheeses curd. We had samples of curd with garlic, dill, hot pepper and with horseradish. We also took some of their processed smoked cheese along. This was something totally new to the Russian consumer. Why would anybody give away cheese unless it wasn't any good? They have never been exposed to this kind of maketing.

They informed me that it would be much more interesting if I would introduce myself and present these samples to the public. I brushed up on my Russian that evening and had no problem giving out a brief synopsis of our new cheese made at the Novy Edem cheese plant right here in the Samara. They were so surprised because they had never met an American, let alone one that spoke Russian. There were hundreds of people employed in this huge office building. We set up our table at the entrance inside the foyer. During the lunch hour it didn't take long for the word to get around that an American was introducing a new cheese product and the samples were free. We even attracted people off the street. We were all very pleased with all the favorable responses that we received. Rimma decided to start producing this product.

It was very labor intensive to produce this cheese because all had to be cut by hand. I informed them I have a machine called a curd mill that cut slabs of curd into the proper sized pieces. In fact I would be willing to donate this machine if they were are really serious about going into production and marketing this product. However, they would have to pay for the custom fees and shipping, which they were very willing to do. The problems with shipping equipment began to haunt me. My American country representative at ACDI-VOCA tried hard to discourage me. They knew many of the circumstance that occur and they more or less said you are on your own. You may never get your money. Because they were so enthusiastic and all the time and effort I spent at this plant, I was very anxious to see them succeed at any risk.

In this situation custom officials require the manufacturers name, the model number, serial number, title of machine, and any other pertinent information. I insisted that it's a used machine and use food equipment rarely brings more than 15% of the original price. They can now go onto the Internet, bring up the manufacturer and put in the model number and serial number and ask for a price quotation. More like $8000 for a new machine. It had been donated to me by Alfred University in Western New York. At one time taught cheese making as part of their food science department. They discontinued the cheese manufacturing part of the program and they asked me if I would take the equipment at no cost. They just wanted the equipment to be used in a cheese plant in the area where some of their former students are now employed. I informed Rimma that she should insist it is a used piece of machinery valued at about $1000.

The deputy director of the Novy Edem plant said we have Russian attorneys that know how to get around the high cost of custom fees. It is not call a curd mill by us. We plan to call it a Russian cabbage cutter and they're worth around $500 new here in Russia. Every factory has a cafeteria for their employees and cabbage is usually on the menu. They also shred cabbage salad. I realized at the time whenever I go to a restaurant I would always get coleslaw because this is something that's very easy and cheap to prepare so everybody had one of these machines called cabbage cutters. This is the information we will feed them. Just let us know the cost of shipping.

When I returned to the states I inquired at Delta airlines how I could ship the curd mill. They said just get a forwarding agent and he will take care of the documentation and paperwork. I asked, "Where can I find a shipping agent?". They said, "Just look in the telephone book". There was one in Williamsville, NY; just a few miles from me. In fact he knew of Kutter's Cheese Factory. He said, "I always stop there and buy cheese", I could pick it up and take it to the airport". I called Delta Airlines and I told them about this piece of machinery. Delta flies from New York to Moscow every day, seven days a week. I told them I would be flying back to Moscow soon. They said we can put it on the same flight that you will be flying on. I wasn't aware that on a commercial flight they actually carry some freight. I thought this would be perfect, I could meet someone from Novy Edem with a vehicle to pick up this piece of machinery.

Meanwhile we had a terrorist attack on 9/11 in New York City. This changed everything including the shipping cost but it only went from $375 to $450, which I thought was still quite reasonable. They put the equipment on a cargo plane that only carried freight because of increased security. It arrived in Moscow several days before I arrived. I couldn't believe that they were going to be able to get it through customs with improper identification and information. However, they succeeded, paying a $75 customs fee. You need Russians who are clever enough to handle these affairs. When I met them at the Moscow airport he paid me $450 for shipping cost in cash. They were so thrilled to get this piece of machinery. They actually drove about 1000 miles with a small Russian car. I said how you are going to get this large crate in your car they brought out a hammer and some tools and took the crate apart. Dismantled the machine into parts, put in the car and left the crate behind then and drove off to Samara.

This was a most interesting project because I felt I had accomplished something and my cheese products will now be produced in another city in Russia. Before my return to Moscow an interpreter invited me to her home for dinner. She was an elderly lady who was an interpreter prior to the fall of communism. Those times you had to be an affiliate of the KGB. She was still reluctant to speak freely about her past experiences.

Rimma Grishina wrote a letter she wanted me to deliver to ACDI-VOVA in Washington, DC commending me for all my time work and donation of machinery. Here is her letter which she translated into English.

When I completed this assignment Grison Vyacheslav presented me with a book about the ten most distinguished enterpreneurs of the post Soviet Era. He was one of the ten men written about. It was a pleasure working with him.

Самарская городская общественная организация инвалидов

"НОВЫЙ ЭДЕМ"

443030, г. Самара,
ул. Чернореченская,6
тел./факс (8462),
41-15-87,41-16-01,41-16-04

р/с 40703810554400100095
в Кировском отд. № 6991 АК СБ РФ,
БИК 043602606, ИНН 6312034479,
к/с 30101810800000000606

Исх. № 17 от 26.01.2001г

Evaluation of the ACDI-VOCA consultant Mr.A.Kutter

The American consultant Mr.Antony Kutter is a very good specialist in manufacturing of hard and process cheese. He has a great experience in this area and manufactures more than 20 varieties of cheeses both traditional and brand products. He studied the technology and the variety of products manufactured at our plant and expressed a high opinion of the process cheeses and cream cheeses. His recommendations concerned widening the variety of process cheeses by using flavouringspopular in the USA like garlic, onion, parsley and dill. As to the hard cheese manufactured by the plant he mentioned that its taste answered the demand of Russian consumers but pointed out that its texture could be improved by using high quality milk.

He also advised on the process of curing hard cheese. Mr.Kutter suggested that we should use vacuum packaging prior to curing in order to prevent mould growth in the curing chamber. At present 15 percent of our hard cheese is rejected because of the flaws and gas formation. The expert explained it not by the violation of technology but by poor milk quality. At the same time he approved of the creative approach of the management staff and chief specialists to the problem. They do not allow any loss of the product but use the blocks of hard cheese having flaws in manufacturing high quality process cheese. We are very thankful to him for his critical approach and valuable advice.

In order to improve the quality of cheese and to conquer the Russian market Mr.Kutter suggested that we should act together with milk producers, we should mention to them the critical points that influence the quality of milk, have seminars on milk quality. Mr.Kutter shared with us the technology of manufacturing cheese curds. Our technologists liked the new product and at the end of the week tasting of the new product took place in the Department of Agriculture of Samara region. Questioning of the consumers showed their approval of the new product.

Now the management of the cheese plant decided to include "Cheese Curds" into their product line. Mr.Kutter is willing to donate curd cutting equipment to Samara cheese plant "New Edem".

At the final meeting with the top management and the General Director of the holding company all the recommendations of the VOCA consultant were listened to with great attention.
Mr.Kutter demonstrated deep knowledge of Russia and its economical problems as he has been to Russia 13 times.
It is extremely important that he is persistently learning Russian and he can make himself understood by his Russian colleagues in the process of cheese making and in different everyday situations.

As a bottom line we want to say that experience and dedication of Mr.Kutter to his assignment at our plant make him a most useful consultant and we would like to work with him again.

Executive Director   Rimma Grishina

103

CURD MILL SHIPPED TO RUSSIA

CHAMPION Curd Mill - 12" Production Size

SPECIFICATIONS

FRAME
Welded stainless steel construction. Tubular stainless steel rails. 1⅝" diameter x 72" long. All corners rounded. No bolts, nuts, rivets or screws are used in the milling zone.

HOPPER AND STRIPPERS
Stainless steel hopper, 11⅛" wide. Heavy stainless steel strippers.

DISC ROLLER
Twenty stainless steel alloy discs 4-11/16" diameter spaced ½" apart. Spacers 1¼" diameter. Discs and spacers easily removed from disc roller shafts by removing the disc roller nuts.

CUTTING KNIFE ASSEMBLY
All welded and machined for close cutting clearances. Cutter knife RPM 370. Standard 3-knife mill cuts cubes ⅜" x ⅜". Mill can also be furnished with two cut-off knives cutting

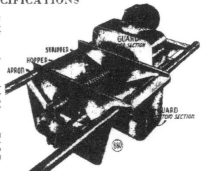

To properly show bronze bearings, clamp plate is not shown. With a quarter turn of the bearings all shafts can be easily lifted from the frame.

15/16" x ⅜" cubes, or four cut-off knives cutting 7/16" x ½" cubes. The third dimension of the cube is governed by the thickness of the matted curd. Cutter knives can also be omitted for Italian types of cheese.

BELT AND GEAR GUARD
All enclosed stainless steel, easily removed from mill.

MOTOR — ½ H.P., single or three phase.

GEARS
Corrosion resistant, aluminum bronze alloy castings.

PULLEYS
Driven pulley 2-groove, 10" diameter. Motor pulley 2-groove, 2¼" diameter.

SHAFT DIAMETERS AT BEARINGS
Disc roller gear side ¾". Disc roller opposite gear side ⅝". Cutter knife both ends ¾".

OUTSIDE WIDTH OVER RAILS — 20¼".

NET WEIGHT — 160 pounds.

SHIPPING WEIGHT — 230 pounds.

CURD MILL TRUCK -- A special curd mill truck is available. This supports the mill along the side of the vat while milling and can be used to carry the mill around the factory. Refer to bulletin 1420-1.

104

Krasnodar Krai and Sochi

My travels and work brought me to Krasnodar Krai. It's one of the most populous southern regions of Russia located on the Kuban River. Krasnodar is the capital it's located near the Black Sea and the Caucasus Mountains. The original name Yekaterinodar meant "Catherine's Gift" in recognition of Catherine the Great.

Once again I met with Nickoli Shergan from Uglish. We traveled to cities of Kurganensk, Kashehable, Lubinsk and Novokubansk. Arrived in Kurganensk, and met with Simon Levonich, head of cheese production at a plant where they made trvorg (Russian Farmers cheese) and processed fluid milk. Simon then took us to Kashehable where they made cheese similar to mozzarella called Salagoony.

We spent three days at this plant working with their personnel in cheddar cheese production and American-style mozzarella. We were able to adapt their equipment and methods to our type of cheese with the same characteristics as we needed to meet our specifications for pizza. This plant was in very bad condition. Milk and sanitary conditions were sadly lacking but with all the drawbacks we were still successful in our production.

Tatyana from Moscow's CNFA office arrived in Kurganensk and the next day we were asked to tour a defunct cheese plant built by Finland just before the collapse of communism. It was built in exchange for crude oil, gas and other natural resources which Russia exported to Finland to finance construction of this modern factory. It had a capacity of 500,000 pounds of milk per day. It could only justify itself under a communist system where all the milk from huge collective farms was available. It was a total automatic Swiss cheese plant, computerized with state of the art equipment. The plant never went into operation with the fall of communism and no subsidies. Another problem is it's owned by the government and they refused to sell it or dismantle it and auction off the equipment. They still feel that some foreign country would start a joint venture and put this plant into operation. This will never happen. There are not enough collective farms not in bankruptcy to be able to provide the milk supply for this plant. It just seems so incomprehensible that a modern state of the art facility will never open.

Next we visited another cheese plant in an adjacent region that was under construction and halted after Perestroika. The plant was 75% completed when communism collapsed in 1991 much of the new equipment is still in shipping crates standing in a warehouse.

Simon wants to finish construction of this plant and would like Nickoli Shergan and me to act as consultants when they start cheese production. I asked Simon about a milk supply. He said this is a smaller operation and after Perestroika there was a decree that no collective farm could slaughter their cattle therefore there appears to be a supply of milk in the area. This plant was never privatized. It is still state owned and of course they are interested in any proposal to undertake a plant, start production and provide employment to a depressed area.

We had a meeting with a group of Russian investors who desire to reopen the plant. This is under consideration at the present time. But as usual I can't foresee in the near future how this problem could be solved and financial arrangements made to make this a reality.

Krasnodar and Cossack History

I found this region thoroughly fascinating. On several occasions visiting cheese factories I would see these people bring milk to the cheese plant. Nickoli Shergen said to me, "can you see those women, how strong and broad shouldered they are, they are Cossacks. They have fertile land, good climate and are people with old traditions that they still cultivate today".

Cossacks undoubtedly were some of the best farmers in Russia. Wheat and corn from the Kuban and Don were one of their chief exports. They had some of the best dairy cattle and they had several breeds of swift saddle horses. Principal farming occupations were dairy cattle, sheep, horse breeding, fishing and hunting; which made the Cossack's prosperous. Their wealth created envy in the masses of the Russian peasantry who were land hungry and often destitute. In addition to the rich black earth so good for farming the land contained riches below the ground.

They were considered one of the most advanced peoples of the Russian Empire. In the years preceding the Revolution of 1917 every Cossack boy and girl received an elementary school education and a great many of them went on to high school or to learn special skills and vocations. There is a Russian proverb, "education is light and ignorance is darkness". It also should be noted that this urge of Cossacks to give their youth an education was frowned upon by the Czar's government. They were repeatedly told that the only education they needed was special military training.

Many did become trained officers of the Cossack regiments. They resented the implication they were needed for military only. They wanted their sons and daughters as teachers, judges, bankers, traders, merchants and priests. Their schools, court offices, factories, shops and churches were the pride of ther communities.

In payment for faithful military service each Cossack clan, by special Imperial grant, received acknowledgment of full ownership over the lands originally conquered and settled by the Cossacks. As rural families were large ,the sons remained in the family till long after the end of their active military service. Upon reaching the age of 17 they received a parcel of land and the larger the family the richer it was in land and number of working hands.

They were conscientious and trustworthy people. Stalin would trust these people to immediately ride off to war to defend their borders. They have rich traditions, folklore and costumes and they perform in dances for entertainment. They are also skilled horsemen. They would respond to the cry, "ON TO THE DON ON TO THE KUBAN!" as sounded by Lenin or Trotsky. Off they would ride to defend their borders.

One of my most cherished possessions is a bronze sculpture cast in Russia in 1875 by "Lanseray" a famous Russian sculptor. It depicts a Cossack riding full speed off to defend his land from intruders. He is reaching down to his wife or girl friend and kissing her good-bye, sometimes never to return. It is called the "Farewell Kiss".

Sochi

In Krasnodar Krai

Simon Levonich, Nickoli Sergan and I traveled to the city of Sochi. It was a six hour trip through the mountains with a lot of hairpin turns on a narrow highway. We never came across any small villages and all along the way there would be people cooking food on charcoal fired grills along the road. I said to Simon lets stop and have something to eat. He said, "I never stop and eat at one of these places, you don't know what they're serving, could be a dog". There are no food inspectors monitoring these cookouts. Many of these Russians were desperately trying to make a living catering to tourists. We finally met up with a friend of his and we stopped and had lunch where he knew what they were serving.

I've always heard about Sochi, a summer resort for Russian people of status in the Communist Party. It is a resort city which sprawls along the shores of the Black Sea and against the background of the snowcapped peaks of the Caucasus Mountains. It has beaches, palms trees, historic architecture and mineral baths. Joseph Stalin established Sochi as a fashionable resort area and had his favorite dacha built here. It is home to many Russian sanatoriums, not like sanatoriums in the US for people with medical problems. In Russia every large industry or ministry had its own sanatorium, where you would go on vacation and just relax and enjoy yourself. It was like a resort in the US. Many times working in Russia instead of staying in a hotel they would let me stay in a sanatorium and I could engage in all the activites. It is a wonderful place to spend a vacation. They also pamper you with massages. Every Russian was eligible upon retirement to go there, very cheap, for fun and relaxation.

Under President Putin the city is witnessing a significant increase in investments. The International Olympic Committee selected Sochi for the Olympic Winter games in 2014 and the organizers are certain that these Winter Olympics will be an unforgettable experience for sports fans worldwide. It has been reported in the the Russian news that it will be one of the most expensive olympics in modern history.

Simon had just purchased a large restaurant in Adler a city along the Black Sea coast adjacent to the Georgia border. There is now some hostility between Russia and Georgia. The border was closed except for people from Georgia who were allowed to bring their tropical fruit and set up stands in Adler just for the day. I tried to take some pictures as people were coming across the border and a policeman put his hand in front of me and said no pictures allowed. This was the first time a border agent threaten to confiscate my camera. I explained to him that I was an American tourist and hadn't taken any pictures and would comply with any of the restrictions. I certainly do not want to break any laws. We exchanged pleasantries and we both went on our way.

Simon's restaurant had been closed. It had been partially damaged by fire. He told me he paid $48,000 and he wanted to turn it into a dairy plant. He wanted to make ice cream and maybe cream cheese. He wanted (CNFA) to authorize my return as a consultant when he starts renovating the building for a food processing dairy facility. He feels that the future is bright because when Russia comes out of this economic crisis this resort will boom. It has had an increase in foreigners arriving during the warm season. It could be a very cosmopolitan center for tourism. However, there is a war going on in Chechnya near Georgia which does affect tourism.

We were asked to make an appointment to visit the Radisson Hotel in Sochi. They were interested in American type cheese, especially cream cheese because they were making cheesecakes and it was so expensive to import from the US. I talked to the chef at the Radisson Hotel and told him about our project in Adler where we could possibly make this cream cheese. Simon said he had made up his mind and he would start construction at this new location.

Simon owned a cottage in Sochi and he invited us to stay for another three days. Nickoli and I spent time relaxing and swimming in the Black Sea. It was October and the water was salty and warm. The beaches were small pebbles. There were warships anchored out in the bay and I asked Nickoli why naval vessels were stationed off the shores of Sochi. He said, "There is a war going on in Chechnya and there are hostilities with Georgia. The authorities are doing everything they can to send a message to the people that this is a safe place to vacation and we are on guard and nothing will happen here". It was an enjoyable three days off work visiting the parks, monuments and tropical gardens. After the third day we went to Sochi Airport and flew back to Moscow.

Sochi Again – All About Corruption

I was always watching the Russian news on television. It was reported they are building a new Italian style building at the Black Sea. It has a fitness center, a hideaway tea house, a concert amphitheater, swimming pools, sports grounds, landscaped parks and a landing pad for three helicopters. It is now under construction and said it had already cost $1 billion. According to a Russian whistleblower, it had been paid for with money donated by a Russian businessman for the use of Prime Minister Vladimir Putin. The funds have come mainly through a combination of corruption, bribery and theft.

News of this place began to leak in 2006 and has never been a subject of speculation until now. No one has reported the details of this corrupt undertaking but we do know for whom it is built. I am sure this will be part of on going construction of roads buildings and sports accommodations for the 2014 Winter Olympics. Russian official are boasting that this winter Olympics will be the greatest Olympics the world will witness. They are anticipating spending upwards of 12 billion dollars.

We seem to be entering a new era of transparency with all our new computer connected information technology. Wiki-leaks has exposed so many secret documents from all over the world. Secret Swiss bank accounts by some Swiss whistle blowers have been exposed. It has always been taken for granted that Swiss bank accounts were held in total secrecy. Even Russia has computer hackers who are now releasing incriminating and classified information. It will be more difficult to keep corruption from being exposed in countries with corrupt governments in future years.

I have never been contacted by Simon Levonich about his venture into the dairy business. Although I think he made it a wise investment in buying that restaurant with the upcoming Olympics. He invited me and my wife to return to Sochi and stay in his summer villa. Maybe someday I'll be able to take a vacation to Sochi, such a beautiful place. You can swim in the Black Sea and a very short distance away is the snow covered peaks of the Caucasus Mountains where you can go skiing.

I remember speaking to the manager of the Radisson Hotel on the Black Sea. "We need to promote Sochi, so few Americans know about how wonderful and magnificent this place is to vacation". He said, "The Radisson Hotel had a booth at an exhibition promoting travel to their worldwide hotels. It was held in the United States and American people approached us in our booth. They would ask where is Sochi? We would say on the Black Sea and they would ask where is the Black Sea? We have to make a greater effort to promote Russia to attract tourists from America. I am sure the Olympic will change all that".

At the time of publishing this book the Winter Olympics have been held. The media has extensively reported about massive corruption and cronyism in the construction of the Russian Olympics. Many of the Russian contractors are associates of Putin.

Original estimates of $10 billion dollars has ballooned into over $50 billion. It is alleged that one third of the cost was siphoned off. I only know what is reported by the media. I'm sure Russia hasn't changed. There is corruption in every country including in our American political system. If I were a Russian I would be proud of Vladimir Putin. He went for the gold to bring the Olympics to Sochi and deserves the gold. Now the world will know where Sochi is. It would be a awesome place for American citizens to vacation.

Vladimir Putin is a patriarch and loves his country. He wants to be recognized on the world stage as an equal power with equivalent status. The time I spent in Sochi left me with many fond pleasant memories. It is Vladimir Putin's show case to the world.

Travel to Krasnodar Region
January 26 – 27, 2003

"Brukhovetsky" Milk Processing Plant
Oblast/Krai Krasnodar

I flew to Philadelphia then on Air France to Paris and then on Delta to Moscow, finally staying overnight at the Aerostar Hotel. On Tuesday I went to the ACDI-VOCA office for briefing and met my translator, Irena Chernova. At 3 PM we left for the Moscow airport and caught a flight to Krasnodar. A driver from the plant picked us up and we drove two hours to the Brukhovetsky Milk Processing Plant. They put us up in a comfortable three room apartment in of the milk processing plant. This is common in Russian where all factories had housing for special guests. There were no hotels in communist days like we find in every suburban community in America.

We took a short walk around the village and bought some groceries and some bottles of Russian wine and returned to our apartment. We made supper and ate some cheese that I brought from the US, had some wine and relaxed after a long flight and drive. Irena really liked the cheese and was quite excited that she was assigned to this project. She told me she had met Nickoli Shergan when I traveled to another region of Krasnodar.

Wednesday the 28th 2003

I arrived at the plant for a tour and was introduced to the directors and chief technologist. It was a large plant with concrete walls surrounding the property with barb wire strung across the top. We toured the facilities. The main part of their operation was production of skim milk powder, butter, tovorog (farmer cheese) and cultured milk products. In former days there wasn't a wide variety of dairy products, basically one kind of hard cheese, one kind of soft cheese, sour cream and fluid milk products.

Sour cream is very popular in Russia but most of the sour cream had a weak body. I would introduce sour cream with different flavors which we refer to as "chip dip", something they were not familiar with. Russians generally don't snack but some how it caught their attention. Sour cream needs a firm body so it will adhere to your potato chips or vegetables. I would show them how we would take a baked potato and layer it with sour cream and it would stand up under the heat. Their sour cream would run off the potato like gravy.

That afternoon Alexander, Irena and I addressed a group of 50 employees. They asked numerous questions pertaining to my cheese operation in America. Then we sampled all the cheese that I carried with me that we manufactured at our US plant. One lady even brought some of her homemade wine to augment our tasting. It was an excellent wine that really complemented our cheese. It created a pleasant cheerful atmosphere for this cheese tasting. Irene and I returned to the apartment and prepared supper. The director of the plant always encouraged us to go to a restaurant. They were willing to pay for our meals, but after always eating in restaurants it becomes tiresome. It's more pleasant to go back to your apartment and prepare your own meals occasionally. After dinner Irena would always help me with my Russian. She was pleased and said we will only speak Russian in the apartment. This is less stressful and doesn't require a high level of vocabulary. When working on assignment it's less demanding if I don't need translating assistance every minute. This gives her an opportunity to make new friends while on assignment.

Saturday

The plant did not operate today. At 9:30 the driver picked us up and took us to a river where they built a huge reservoir for irrigation. This area of Russia is like the San Joaquin Valley of California. It is very warm in the summer and the soil is black and very deep, a very productive agricultural region. I saw lots of winter wheat growing in huge fields. We went on to Krasnoyarsk to an outdoor market where I bought a fur hat like all the Russians wear in the wintertime. Then we went to dinner. From there we went to a museum depicting the history and life in Krasnodar.

We returned to the apartment and Irena, Lyudmila, I and several other employees went to a banya. The women went in first and then the men. Everyone kept a towel wrapped tightly around and we all sat in the warm steam room just relaxing, drinking tea and some vodka. The conversation was warm and the atmosphere was congenial. I always wish this tradition was practiced here in America.

Sunday

Our driver Anatoly picked us up at 10:30 AM. We drove around the village briefly then we went to his house for dinner. They had a beautiful home, four families got together and had a four unit condo built. The inside reminded me of houses in Germany with tiles and decorations. I have never been treated to such an array of food. We stayed until 7:30 PM and I was just tired from trying to converse in Russian. It really gave Irena a break when we could all talk in Russian and she doesn't have to stop and translate every last word. It gives her an opportunity to just be one of us at a party. What a great feeling!

Irena really enjoyed this assignment. She was a new employee of ACDI-VOCA and hoping to familiarize herself will all aspects of the dairy industry. She had a flawless command of the English language. She said she liked the variety of cheese that I brought to introduce to everyone at the milk plant and this was a totally new experience for her

All of our make proceedures and results were recorded. They now have the technology to produce this cheese.

Recommendations
1) Select cheese curd, cottage cheese and sour cream products with flavors (chip and salad dressings) for future new products.
2) Set up a Research and Development Department within the Laboratory. Begin to perfect these new products. Experiment with different cultures and stabilizers. Determine the proper acid and moisture contents to achieve favorable results.
3) Purchase a small vat and some packaging materials.
4) In house engineers could fabricate much of the hand utensils and packaging equipment. I could advise them on these matters.
5) Contact spice and ingredient manufacturers and ask for samples of their products. The culture they presently use could be used for the new products.
6) Some time in the future milk quality issues should be addressed. I have experience in farm sanitation because I was responsible for the quality of milk received in our plant in the US. I could help them with this.
7) Have ACDI-VOCA provide an American farmer who produces milk to advise the farm directors on the procedures required by our department of agriculture for the production of milk.
8) Possibly in the future set up a farmer and processor association whereby seminars are conducted to resolve mutual problems so both can produce a highly marketable food product.
9) Develop some new marketing ideas. I would be able to discuss many of our marketing ideas in the US.
10) If there is any money available for repairs my priority would be to repair floors.

ACODEK

Borisoglesk Russia

I received a call from my office in Moscow for yet another assignment. There was a request to travel to a company called ACODEK, part of Agribusiness Management Company L.L.C. and Affiliate of America First Corp. located in Omaha, Nebraska with offices in Moscow. They own several food plants in Russia and were having production, quality and I assume, some financial problems.

I flew back to Moscow and met with Alexander Afanasiev, the general director and Tanya Shinkarenko an investment analyst for their Moscow office. She spoke fluent English and it was very enjoyable working with her. It was the first time in Russia that I ever encountered an operation that was owned by limited partners in the US. I have heard of investors who have this kind of investment in their portfolio. Limited partnership consists of two or more persons with at least one general partner and the rest limited partners.

Tanya and I traveled to the cheese plant which was several hours out of Moscow. We were discussing financial problems. My first thought was why are your offices in Moscow. It is so expensive just renting office space. Why not have yoru office at the cheese plant? She told me you are not recognized as somebody with creditability if you don't have an office in Moscow. Immediately a flag went up about their financial conditions.

We stayed in a children's camp. It was in the winter but was still open. There was a cafeteria open everyday for its workers so I would eat with them and we had many interesting conversations. I remember several times that I would go cross-county skiing in the birch forests surrounding this camp.

At the plant I met with Director Mikhail Sorokeen and the chief technologist and production officer Natalie. (can't recall her last name)

This is my second trip to ACODEK cheese Plant in Borisoglesk. Mikhal decided that we should experiment with cream cheese. It was my idea to make some processed cheese. There were problems with undergrade posad cheese (Russian type gouda) that had been returned from customers. It would make sense to process this cheese and sell it at a profit.

Cream cheese

I brought with me some Philadelphia brand cream cheese. I brought all the stabilizers and the formulations to make it in the laboratory and train lab personnel I needed a homogenizer or at least a very high-pressure pump to finish off the product. This equipment was not available so we improvised the best we could. With some unorthodox procedures we were able to produce a product similar to our U.S. samples.

We also made a cream cheese spread and added Russian fruit flavors and some American dill seasoning.

The plant workers were delighted with these samples, however management personal found them unacceptable. In the U.S. many people are looking for reduced fat products. They accept low fat products because butter contains 80% fat whereas cream cheese products can go as low as 20% fat. After receiving mixed reviews I think we should look at some other options

All my comments and criticism are of a constructive nature. I have the welfare of the employees and the facilites at heart. They must not hesitate to make improvements.

I suggest the purchase of a process cheese cooker. I saw one at the food machinery show in Moscow. The cost was $5,000 and it was Russian made. This would give the plant versatility to broaden their product line. A homogenizer would be helpful if you want to make cream cheese.

There isn't any reason ACODEK cannot make any variety of cheeses they choose. We also have to think about marketing and promotion. I think Russians wants better cars, more home improvements and a tastier food supply. It's only human nature, so let us be an innovator in the cheese business.

Meeting at Agribusiness LP Moscow

I have had several meetings with Tanya discussing management problems. How we will implement them are still being decided. My discussions with her were based mainly on plant restructuring, new product development and new management. These are a few of the ideas we discussed:

      A   Eliminate offices in Moscow and move them to the cheese plant.

      B   Reduce number of employees

      C   Determine the qualifications for plant director and how we can consolidate management

D	responsibility with chief technologist.
D	Direct product distribution from manufacturing facility.
E	Develop new products to broaden product distribution
F	New method of payment of milk based on protein levels

Ukraine

I received an invitation from OlgaTutarinova of Rich Products in Russia to attend a social at the Ukranian Hall in Buffalo, NY. We have many Ukrainian immigrants living in the western New York area and the Canadian Niagara region. After having worked with the Mennonites in Siberia, many of whom had Ukrainian ancestry, I became interested in their history. At the Ukranian Hall I met Vadim Sukmanov who asked me would I also consider doing volunteer work for the dairy industry in his country

CNFA Washington DC, Office: I Spoke with William Witting, director, of agricultural volunteer program they call me and asked if I would accept an assignment in the Ukraine. Before I accepted I thought I would do a little research about the country of Ukraine.

Some key facts about Ukraine:

The official language is Ukrainian, however, I've heard Russian spoken in the eastern part of Ukraine. In western Ukraine the main church is the Ukrainian Greek Catholic Church which does not strongly pledge allegiance to the Pope. In the western part of Ukraine, possibly because it borders Poland, there are many Roman Catholics. The Romanian language I am told was similar to Russian, however, I could not understand them but they could understand my Russian.

I recall at the time I was working there Pope John Paul was visiting Ukraine. He was the most traveled Pope in history and his dream was to travel to Moscow. He never succeeded in receiving an invitation to Moscow but he was able to visit the Ukraine. I remember when I was in the Ukraine I was working in Lviv and Kiev. There were signs welcoming Pope John Paul everywhere in the western part of Ukraine, however, in the eastern part of Ukraine there was hardly any mention of his visit. In fact there was no welcoming committee or ceremony when he arrived at the airport in Kiev.

Leonid Kuchma was elected president in one of the first peaceful elections after the collapse of the Soviet Union. There are still many Russian sympathizers. I remember going to street rallies where everything was in Russian. They were marching with signs, "Ukraine without Kuchma". They were always peaceful.

Project: Zaporizhia Agrodvir Dairy Development Program

Host organization;   Agrodvir dairy (Agro Plant)
Location: Zaporizihia Oblast Southeast Ukraine

I flew to New York and on to Paris then I caught a flight to the Kiev. It is the only time on any of my assignments where they lost my luggage. There were at least 20 people without their luggage and it finally caught up with me four days later. I wrote to the airline for some compensation or a free ticket but to no avail. I was picked up by my driver we went to the CNFA office to meet the staff for briefing. We drove to the Agro dairy, had dinner and met the owner, Ihor Oleksiv.

Agro Dairy was established as a private company in 1998. It owns the Vesele Dairy Processing Plant, Zaporizhzhia Oblast, equipped with German and Russian production lines. Agrodvir plans to increase the amount of separated milk they process per month.

After I reviewed what they expected as a volunteer for this assignment I thought it was a rather tall order. Ihor Olesksiv said you are just the person to fulfill this project. But, as usual, the owner turns everything over to the production people. He has absolutely no knowledge of agriculture or agri business. That's the last I saw him until weeks later when he drove me to a new plant they purchased. I finished my project and we were to have a final farewell meeting with the staff. We all waited for three hours and the owners never showed. They called and said they were at a meeting and would come after their meeting. I was quite disturbed and I left because I had to pick up my wife at the airport.

She was meeting me and I wanted to spend a week touring the Ukraine on my own time . This assignment was not well managed. I remember I stayed in a hotel in Lviv and many times my driver would be late picking me up. Or no one would be scheduled to be at the plant to work. However, I thoroughly enjoyed working with these people and I really felt we made a lot of progress and they were all very grateful for my time and effort.

I have been accustomed to many delays and this transition from a command economy to a free market economy just doesn't happen overnight, especially with older workers who have lingering gratifing memories of the old communist system where you are instructed what to do and not relay on your intuition.

Trudy *(my wife arrives in Kiev)*

After my assignment was completed I had made arrangements for Trudy to meet me in the Ukraine. She flew to Amsterdam and then on to the Ukraine. They also lost her luggage and finally it caught up to her four days later. She wasn't too happy wearing the same clothes for four days. CNFA provided me with a young man as my interpreter. Visiting all the famous historic sites in the city it would've been great for him to accommodate us as a guide. He was getting paid for his services but he had a girlfriend and he spent more time with her than with us. With my Russian and Trudy's German, we were able to enjoy Lviv and Kiev.

The grand and beautiful medieval city of Lviv is where Trudy and I stayed during my work at Agro. What I remember most about this city was it's cobblestone streets. The small Russian cars with small wheels would travel over these stones and it would really take a toll on them. Cars would literally shake apart till the wheels came off. Trudy and I had a great many lasting memories of this beautiful city and the Ukrainian people.

My Work in the Ukraine

I brought with me twenty varieties of cheese and other dairy products manufactured at my plant in the United States. Also all the ingredients from cultures, rennet, stabilizers and flavorings. All the directors and personnel were there to view and taste and examine the various types of cheeses. All the types were discussed in detail as to their possibility of being produced by AGRO Dairy. There was much interest shown because many types were very new to them. I informed them if they wish to improvise some equipment in the plant we could demonstrate production methods. We traveled to dairy # 1 where they produce yogurt and sour cream. We met the chief engineer, Podon. Also head of production and chief accountant, Ludmela and the production manager Valentine. They were very interested in making American style cottage cheese. We toured the plant and found a vat suitable for this. I wanted to stay at this location and show them the make procedure but my schedule called for me to return that evening to Lviv. Then we discussed the make procedure for cottage cheese. We went into the cheese room and we selected a cheese vat and made some improvements on the equipment. I left them my culture and rennet. I am sure they will be successful. If they have a problem I will still be available by email.

There appears to be problems with the body of the yogurt and sour cream. They were interested in the stabilizers that we use to give our sour cream a heavy body. Their yogurt was very thin, more like a drinkable beverage. We discussed different formulas and their application to improve the product.

There was no proper lab equipment to analyze sour cream or

yogurt. It is important to do a pH test for acidity. There was no Ph meter available. I was able to prepare a formula for sour cream and demonstrate how to make a heavy-bodied sour cream. I also left them one of our formulas for yogurt to improve the body.

AGRO Dairy #2

We drove to dairy #2. They make a Dutch type of cheese like Gouda but in a square shape. We toured the plant and processing facilities. The plant is old and badly in need of basic repairs to the floors, windows, piping etc. It is difficult to keep this facility clean and reduce air borne contamination. The cheese in the curing rooms that I tasted did not have a consistent flavor or texture. However, the cheese that I had presented to me was very tasty. It meets the needs and tastes of the Ukrainian consumer. They indicated to me that 80% of the milk was sub-standard. Because of a deficit milk supply they need to purchase more milk it to fill their orders. There were no reliable methods of checking for quality of milk or finished products. I had with me some material for testing milk for bacteria and trained their personnel in our methods of milk testing.

We made some American style muenster cheese in the laboratory. The milk was over pasteurized and some of the protein destroyed. This gave it a weak body. We also tried to use their culture and rennet and still had poor results. This was a real indication to me that we have some real milk quality problems. I would like very much to travel to collective farms and access the operations and find out where we need to correct deficiencies. I hope to accomplish this at a future time. I can't stress the need to improve overall milk supply.

I returned to this plant and we made processed cheese and cheese spread. Again there wasn't any pH meter or a fast and accurate method of testing for moisture. Everthing was done by guess work. However we made some very good products. We added dry onion and garlic flavors to the spreads. What is important is that we made it out of under grade cheese. This will enable AGRO to utilize poor cheese. With the poor milk it is inevitable they will have under grade cheese. If this plant produces this cheese it would enhance their profitability.

AGRO Dairy #3

We drove to dairy #3. This was a very large plant built in Soviet times and designed to produce a huge amount of swiss cheese. They wanted to make new varieties of cheeses. We proceeded to make a muenster and cheddar cheese curds. We were very happy with the results because of the problems we had at dairy #2. The cheese was very good. We made three flavors, plain, garlic, chive and dill. Several of the workers actually brought fresh herbs from their home gardens. I felt that the staff was very pleased with the results because they learned the actual make procedure.

Next I showed them how to perform analytic tests for quality of raw milk and finished cheese products. They have never experienced using these techniques with our lab supplies.

I discussed with Bogdan (one of the owners), about the importance of cleanliness of equipment. It had heavy deposits of milkstone minerals on the surface. I suggested they use acid cleaners. They felt it was too expensive. I instructed them on recycling of the acid cleaner and how we use ours over again to reduce costs.

Earlier in my Assignment Scope of Work it indicated that AGRO owners felt that there was much room for improvement in their cheese taste especially swiss cheese. It was bitter compared to cheese imported from Switzerland and the Netherlands. I had with me some of our aged swiss produced in my plant. Bogdon commented that he like liked it. The director indicated they had trouble with hole development. Swiss is the most difficult cheese to produce. The eye formation (holes) is very important. The swiss cheese was in 8O Lb blocks and they were not aged enough to cut. They were reluctant to show it to me. They were more interested that I show them how to make new kinds of cheese. They had all the milk prepared for me. Bogdon joined us and every one was pleased with the results.

Recommendations for AGRO
1) In the future there should be some kind of progress made toward improving milk through the inner action of milk producers and cheese processors association. Input should also come from inspectors and regulations from agencies in the government. This will unite parties who have a common goal to bring Ukrainian agricultural standards up to their European counterparts.
2) Set up a department in the plant or a laboratory where new products are developed.
3) Make cheese spread where undergrade cheese can be utilized.
4) Produce a heavy body sour cream and yogurt by dual homogenization or use of stabilizers.
5) Equip labs with the latest tests for milk (coli, drugs and bacteria)
6) The plant needs repairs to floors, windows and piping. I observed birds flying in the plant and bird droppings on the equipment.
7) Consult with technicians from various companies selling ingredients and dairy supplies for the cheese industry.
8) There are much mineral deposits on equipment. This

harbors thermoduric bacteria which survives pasteurization. These bacteria will spoil dairy products. Inquire about cleaning chemicals from companies selling them.

9) I strongly feel we need product improvement. In the next decade competition in the market place will increase. We need to strengthen our position or we will fall by the wayside.

10) If new products are developed I could help them with marketing techniques and strategy that we have found to be successful in our operations. I will share with them how we try and capture a share of the cheese market in the US.

Return to Russia

Volgada Milk Processing Plant

Valadimir Vasilievich Director

I had a very preliminary observation of the facilities. After a lengthy conversation I took a tour of the plant and observed their cheese operations. They are fluid milk processors and soft products such as sour cream and Tvorog. They have gotten into hard cheeses to broaden their product line in hopes of increasing their profits.

They hope to gain some technology in more foreign varieties of cheese. In 1998 I made three trips to Russia to work and travel with Nickoli Shergan. The idea was to train him in the methods of making American style cheese such as cheddar, cheese curds, mozzarella, processed cheese and cheese spread. He would then disseminate the technology in cheese plants in Russia. They informed me that they had purchased the technology for mozzarella from his firm.

They are interested in my assisting them in making processed cheese. I will return in the autumn and begin this project and will also be discussing new type of cheese products.

We will be doing some quality upgrading in their lab procedures and analysis of finished products to help solve quality problems. We haven't formulated our goals and objectives yet. I was only in Volgada for one full day. I had to return to Moscow to catch the plane to the US

Tony Kutter

Lotoshino   Project #331361   Feb 5-2003

I met with the officials at the city administration in Lotoshino and was told this area once produced a famous cheese prior to the Bolshevik Revolution. Somehow the technology was lost. They were very interested in my cheese making expertise to develop a cheese at the plant. They invited Tatyana Mehaylova, milk plant director and Boris, the director of marketing to this meeting.

I brought with me about twenty varieties of dairy products that were manufactured at my US plant. We tasted each kind and discussed how to produce it. They selected several type which they felt were unique. They wanted a new cheese that eventually would develop a good reputation representing this region.

We discussed actual make procedures and they recorded the information. Afterwards we drove to the plant and toured the facilities. I believe we could use their existing equipment to make this cheese. If they are able to establish a market I could advise them on packaging equipment for the product.

They assured me they definitely would pursue making cheese. Had only one day to discuss all the issues involved. I believe they are a potential client for ACDI- VOCA in the near future and I would be happy to return there in April.

I would like to thank especially Elena Rubtsova and Nicholi Kieev and everyone at ACDI-VOCA for this opportunity to work on this project.
Tony Kutter

The Republic of Mordovia Russia

April 20, 2005 (Return for another assignment)

Ojso Dairy Processing Plant, Mechta

Isaev Alexander Arkadievich, Director
Kulagina Maria Nikoleavna, Chief Technologist

The Mordovia Republic is located in the eastern part of Russia. And its capital is Saransk.

The holding company Mechta is managed by Sergei Ivanovich Siushou, the general director and owner. Mechta currently employs 45 people. The enterprise has progressive management eager to offer new cheese products to the local market and increase the overall profitability of the holding company. It now produces butter products, whole milk products, sour cream, tvorog (farmer's cheese) and other low-fat milk products. My project entails me to introduce new hard cheese products and processed cheese spreads.

Most of the equipment at the plant is very new and it was made in Hungary and Germany. The company distributes its cheese and milk products throughout its own stores and Poselok, Chamzinka and Komsomolskoye Mordovia, and in the neighboring cities of the Volga region.

September 4, 2005 Monday.
I arrived in Moscow

September 5th

I had a briefing at ACDI-VOCA and departed for Saranks by overnight train. I arrived in Saranks the next morning and went to the city of Chamzinka. They were very interested in my US cheese operation and how we manufacture, market and distribute our cheese. Also how do we analyze our products to maintain strict quality control and consistency

I had with me cultures, rennet, emulsifiers flavorings and etc, basically this was a cheese maker to cheese makers exchange which made it most interesting. It was one of my most interesting projects and a learning experience for me as to how Russia operates cheese plants and some of the obstacles they face.

They were so iinterested to have somebody from the US visit them who has his own cheese factory and would come to their plant. I worked with their cheese makers side by side on a first name basis exchanging ideas. I recorded some of the questions they asked me.

ANTHONY WHY DID YOU DECIDE TO VISIT US? Could you tell us about your production in the USA?

It is a rare opportunity for in an American to work with the Russian cheese industry. This is my 26th visit to your country with the help of ACDI-VOCA. The main purpose of this program is a farmer to farmer exchange. I took part in building a cheese plant in Omsk, Russia, helped with starting of production in Samara. All my visits have nothing in common with politics. ACDI-VOCA recommended me as a prospective volunteer that could address all these issues.

2) WHAT IS YOUR FIRST IMPRESSION?

I am surprised, first of all that in such a compact area your people are able to produce such a wide variety of products. I always said that Russia has a great potential. I have been to farms in Semenovskoe. I was glad to see your farms. They are healthy animals, which produce a good quality milk. It was explained to me that half of your raw milk comes from Semenovskoe.

I helped my father, a cheese maker, when I was only 14 years old. I have been working in our family cheese plant for 57 years and now I am 72 years old, and the owner of the plant. Our cheese is sold throughout the United States, Puerto Rico, Taiwan and also it is now produced by several Russian cheese plants. Certainly I will learn something communicating with your cheesemakers.

3) HAVE YOU TASTED UBIMUJ GOROD PRODUCTS? WHICH PRDUCTS OF OURS DO YOU LIKE MOST?

Rjazhenka (fermented milk drink) is delicious. We have little of such a product in America, sorry to say. I like almost all the Russian cream cheese with fruit: In producing this product you are more successful than Americans. I have taken this formula for Russian cream cheese and am now producing it in our plant in America. We made it on a small scale for our local trade at our cheese store. Needless to say: our customers are enjoy this product and we will continue its production. I am so fortunate to meet so many people in the Russian cheese industry and share ideas and comments

Travel to Volgograd

Milk Processing Plant   Oblast / Krai: Volgograd Russia
Key facts about Volgograd Russia:

The city was originally called Tsaritsyn, later renamed Stalingrad by Joseph Stalin and now is called Volgograd. This city has been memorialized in remembrance for its turning point in the Second World War for the defeat of the Nazis. When the Germans attacked Stalingrad the primary task was to secure the oil fields in the Caucasus and to do this Stalingrad had to be conquered and the final target was to take Baku and the oil fields.

I can always remember my father would listen intently to the news on the radio about the war in Stalingrad. I was nine years old. So many of my uncles were now fighting in the German army. I look back now after talking to the Russian people, we Americans have never experienced such horrible conditions on our home front. I can still remember my relatives in Germany telling me some of the german prisoners of war never returned home until years after the war was over. There are numerous monuments and memorials commemorating the battle in Stalingrad.

A man said we defeated the Germans and now they live 20 times better than we do. This is such a rich country why do we live so poorly, asked one of my Russian colleagues. He said to me, "if you study our history, we build great things and we destroy everything time and time again".

I was in Russia many times when they celebrated the end of the Second World War. many of these elderly gentlemen would parade in full uniform with all their medals. The Russian government today urges schoolchildren to celebrate Russian victories.

A tour guide said the feeling of patriotism remains loyal because the city suffered so much. We can't forget what happened. This is a city where every piece of ground is soaked in blood.

I am a Korean war veteran. We in America have a national holiday called Memorial Day in commemoration of all the soldiers that died in all the wars in American history. Hardly anyone in America celebrates the end of the Second World War. If I were a Russian combat veteran I would be proud to participate in a memorial service commemorating their victory. They paid such a heavy price for their bravery.

Arrived from Moscow by plane to Volgograd. At the airport I was met by my host and interpreter. We drove by car on some very bumpy roads to Kamyshin, a 3 hour drive. There I met the Executive Director Alexander Dolmatov, Chief technologist Tatiana Tolokova and Financial Manager Tatiana Litvinova.

The Volgograd Oblast is a rich agricultural region I noticed some of the land was under irrigation. What interested me most was that they started a Volgograd Private Farmers Association of about 9000 private farmers in the region. I always preferred to associate with private farmers rather than the directors of huge collective farms. We at ACDI-VOCA always try and encourage private farming.
The company's brand name is "Lyubimya Gorod" (favorite city) which is well known in the area for its quality of their dairy products.

Before I returned to Moscow we had a meeting to discuss and finalized our achievements and our project. They handed me a series of questions that I would comment on and give my honest opinion.

Questions for Anthony Kutter
1. Your evaluation of our products as to its quality. What about our equipment? Do you suggest any modification to improve our processing ability?

2. Do you suggest any changes in the technology or the process to improve the quality of our products?

3. After taste testing our products would you suggest changes in the way we make our products?

4. Do you have any ideas how to utilize our by-products, whey and buttermilk?

5. Any suggestion about the need for quality milk and how important it is to make quality cheese?

6. Is it important to have better equipment? Can we find better equipment that is not too expensive?

7. What do you think about the plant we use for cheese making? Do you have any suggestions about our layout of plant?

8) Please evaluate our cooling equipment and it's efficiency.

9) What do you think of the quality of our incoming milk?

10). Have you visited our supply farms? Would you approve the milk for cheese making?

I tried to answer the questions as they were interpreted. The translation seemed somewhat vague to me when translated word for word. After each question there was a discussion that led to other questions not related to original question. I tried to record this discussion in my memory and then jot these notes for this book. This question and answer session was held at a farewell dinner . The next day I left for the Moscow office for debriefing and to write my final report.

The Republic of Mari-El - *My Next Destination*

Mari-El Republic is a fascinating place to visit for outdoor sportsmen. It is, comparable to our state of Minnesota, weather wise and where visitors can enjoy boating, horseback riding, fishing and mushrooming in the woods. There are also many museums of Natural History and fine arts.

In the Soviet era, Mari-El was closed to foreign travelers and businessmen due to the high share of the military industrial complex, It was opened only in the early 90's

Recruitment Note: This project is designed for volunteer Anthony Kutter. He indicated a strong desire to return to Russia and complete this assignment. Please contact him and start processing.

Sernurskiy Cheese Plant

Cheese Assortment Development

I. Project Information

A. Project Number: HQ #: 331417   Field #: MAV297
B. Project Location: Country: Russia Oblast/Krai: Mari-El
October 28, 2003

E. Starting-Ending date of the assignment:
Start: January 18, 2004   End: January 31, 2004

A. HOST

Name:	Sernurskiy Cheese Plant
Primary Contact:	Dvoretskov Nikolay Mikhailovich, Director
Address:	425450 Mary-El Republic, Sernur
	Zacodskaya St., 8A
Primary Contact:	Vladimir Tarasovich Kozhanov, General
Director	
	Irina Nikolaevna Petrushinskaya, Deputy
Director	
Address:	Mary-El Republik, Yoshkar-Ola Shuseva
	St.,4

I flew to Moscow and was picked up by my driver and taken to Areostar Hotel. The next morning I was briefed at ACDI-VOCA office. That evening I caught night train to Yoshkar-ola, arriving in the morning. The driver took me to the city of Sernur. I stayed in a private house, like a bed and breakfast.

The Sernurskiy Cheese Plant is located in the city of Sernur. It is one of the biggest cheese plants in the Mari-El Republic and is mainly involved in hard and processed cheese production. The Sernurskiy Cheese plant was founded in 1973 as a state dairy processing company. In 2001 it was reorganized into a joint-stock company. The company's main products include smoked processed cheese ("kolbasnyi") and following types of hard cheeses:
- poshekhonskiy;
- kostromskoi;
- radonezhskiy;
- rossiyskiy;

The cheese production operation employs a total of 138 people. The equipment is mostly domestically-made, and consists of the following pieces: four vats with 5 tons capacity each, six vertical presses, a smoking chamber, and two automated packaging machines for different kinds of cheese in foil and plastic.

The Sernurskiy Cheese plant has recently expanded its processing operations. But the plant still uses only 82% of its capacity. The Company's top management would like to fully utilize the capabilities of the facility, expand the product line of hard and processed cheese and fine-tune the production processes in order to reduce the cost of production.

In-country activities/tasks:

The volunteer will complete the following activities in-country:

- meet with the company's general director and main specialists to become familiar with the company's operations, current needs and plans;
- observe and evaluate cheese production operation and review the technological processes which are currently in place;
- determine the potential for producing new hard and processed cheese products;
- provide hands-on training in hard and processed cheese-making and product formulation, as well as in product research and development;
- assist in producing new hard and processed cheese items;
- help improve the quality of the hard and processed cheese currently produced using the available equipment

Jan 18 to Jan 31, 2004

At the Semurskiy Cheese Plante we met with Nikoli Dvoretskov, Director of the cheese plant and Valerie Koshanov, chief technologist, and toured the facilities. It was quite modern. The building had been renovated and a new expansion was developed adjacent to the original processing area. The equipment was old, from former communist times, but adequate and sanitary. I was impressed because in my seven years of working in Russian cheese factories this was one of the best facilities. They also had a well-trained dedicated work staff.

We tasted all the different varieties of cheese products they produce. They were tasty. In general they met all the standards acceptable to the Russian consumer. The incoming milk supply was graded into three different categories of quality, usually by the acidity of milk. There were no daily standard plate counts, direct microscopic counts or cell counts for mastitis that I was aware of. Some of the farms lack refrigerated cooling. This milk is brought to the plant for cooling and stored in tanks to ripen naturally and comingled with other milk. Some of the low quality milk was used for tvorog, which requires high acidity. Also there was no testing for penicillin inhibitory drugs.

In the US the department of Agriculture and Markets sets requirements for milk quality. This makes it much simpler for the cheese manufacturer to produce a consistent quality cheese.

From sampling the cheese I detected different textures and flavors from the different milk quality. Some bitterness but this is not a problem to overcome when making processed cheese. This is an area we hope to expand with development of processed cheese with seasonings, herbs and spices.

I did not have access to collective or individual farms. I feel this is where it all begins with making quality cheese. I am proposing some ideas to ACDI-VOCA on how we could follow American and European Agricultural regulations. We need to bring the milk processor and the milk producer together.

My scope of work now is to introduce new types of cheese and dairy products, marketing ideas, more attractive packaging and many new applications in the laboratory for analyzing our products and raw milk supplies. Another problem is utilization of whey and how to dispose of it without harming the environment.

My objective is to meet with the general director and the main specialists of the cheese facility and become familiar with operations. I will share with them the latest technology, our production methods; make procedures for natural and processed cheeses and soft dairy products such as cottage cheese and sour cream products.

ACCOMPLISHMENTS - Sernurskiy Cheese Plant

We had several key personnel taste all my varieties of cheese. After sampling each cheese we reviewed make procedure. Several items where chosen for experimental production. Cheddar cheese curd, a snack food item, took preference; also processed cheese with different flavors was of great interest. Next they wanted to make a heavy bodied sour cream. I introduced sour cream with various flavors that we refer to as "chip-dip" in America. I had recipes for salad dressings made from sour cream and mayonnaise. Different sorts of dressings for salad are an American tradition readily acceptable in Russia.

We set up an area in the plant where we experimented making some of the new products. We made several cheeses using my cultures and also Russian cultures. The cheese turned out very good. This is an opportunity to experience the actual make procedure. Next we made processed cheese in their cheese cooker. Again I had all the emulsifiers and whey powder that I needed to complete the process. We used different formulas using both my ingredients and Russian ingredients. We made sour cream using my stabilizers to obtain a heavy body sour cream. This is important if you want it for dipping potato chips or vegetables. If it is too thin it will drip off when dipping with snacks.

Another cheese of interest was cottage cheese, a much sweeter version than Russian tvorog. Cottage cheese has been introduced in the Moscow area where it is gaining in popularity.

In the laboratory I demonstrated new simplified techniques for running standard plate counts on raw milk. It determines the actual bacteria in the milk to determine quality. Coliform and coli test were performed and we determined the degree of post contamination in the finished products. They indicated that they have never seen or heard of these methods. All in all the products were clean. We found small but acceptable amounts of coliform in the sour cream. By American standards the state inspector would inform us and it would necessitate immediate correction. I trained personnel as to how we would take line samples and find the area where the problem existed.

I took with me some attractive packaging material. They had a vacuum machine so we were able to show how modern packaging ideas can capture the eye of the consumer. This was sort of a seminar in what the future holds for the dairy industry in Russia.

SUMMARY   FINAL REPORT   Sernurskiy cheese plant

Then we can adopt all the latest technology and understand the following:
> a) Milk Composition/ Standardization: Influence of casein-to-fat ratio. Total solids, lactose and mineral content in the finished product, consequently these factors affect moisture levels and acid development in cheese.
> b) Rate of acid development, leads to variations in the composition, color and physical properties.
> c) Aging and curing: Important reactions like proteolysis and microbial growth occur here. This affects salt, lactose and Ph levels crucial to texture and flavor development.
> d) Currently there is some competetion from alternate non-dairy fat cheese substituted with vegetable oils. This occurred in the US but was a failure due to lack of taste. It will not be a factor in Russia's future in my opinion.

March 15 2004
This was an article in a Russian Newspaper in Oscarlar, Mary-El Republic about the Sernursky cheese facility.

A leader in Russian Agriculture. That is how Minister of agriculture praised Vladimir Kozhanov, director of YTK Holding Company.

He met with American consultant from ACDI-VOCA. Anthony Kutter. He visited the Sernursky Cheese Plant by invitation of the VTK holding Company. The main conversation was about milk production in the Mari-El republic and the situation as it presents itself and some of the problems we must overcome.

Mr. Anthony Kutter is a specialist in cheese manufacturing with 52 years of experience. He shared his technology with the directors of holding company. The American told about the present state of agriculture and cheese production in the US. Also how his company operates and manufactures different varieties of cheese. He stated that much of his technology was formulated over his 52 years in business. Alexander Egosheen noted that there wasn't that much time available for him and tell about his work and planning to help agriculture in his republic.

The American was quite surprised about the availability of low cost loans to farmers. Also low cost electricity was available for certain dairy producers. This is a real tribute to the minister of agriculture and his department. A step in the right direction Tony said.

Alexander Egosheen said he returned from a trip to Canada on a fact-finding commission to improve and increase the efficiency of the Russian dairy industry. There is a need to improve transportation of raw milk. Each farmer brings his milk in small tank trucks. These trucks are made of aluminum and not up to standards. New stainless steel tankers are needed and we must devise a system of collection.

There needs to be a new formulation to regulate the price of milk to promote a fair profitable return to farmers. This would be beneficial to the whole economy in the Mari-El republic. This would spur an increase in milk production.

He promised support to agriculture in every way. He praised Mr. Kutter for his deep understanding of all the problems in the Russian dairy industry especially in Mari-El. Tony has traveled to many parts of Russia and has an insight to the uniqueness of Russia. Alexander Egosheen stated that in dynamic ways we hope to adopt the latest western technology to develop agriculture in Mari-El so we will become more competitive and become a leader in the dairy industry in Russia.

Tony Kutter, American consultant meeting President of Mari-El
Republic of Russia at the Sumursky Cheese Factory

My Final Report

Invariably whenever I left Russia after completing an assignment
Vladimir Soldatenkov, my project manager, would inquire when I
would be available to return. We will never find a volunteer who built
two cheese plants in Russia and has developed a cheese operation
in the US that manufactures such a wide variety of cheese and dairy
products. We have a request from Perm, Russia for a volunteer to
help them in the cheese industry. After completing my assignment I
was actually very anxious to return home to my family and catch up
on many business projects that I put on hold at the cheese factory. I
started doing research on Perm, an area of Russia that most
Americans including myself had never heard of.

Vladimir said to me ,"We have enough projects for you that will
take you all the way across Russia to Vladivostok which is an eight
hour flight out of Moscow. Russia truly is an immense country with so
many different ethnic peoples and many languages. At the time of
my writing this book I never reached the far eastern part of Russia's
Vladivostok. In the next few chapters I will be writing about my
experiences and adventures along the Mongolian border.

The Soviets did an excellent job of keeping foreigners out of the
city of Perm. Most people from outside the city simply did not know
of its existence at the time or even that there were one million

citizens living in Perm until the end of the Cold War. Perm did not appear on certain Soviet-made maps, not even the roads towards Perm were printed. The city was a fortress where huge military industries existed. Nowadays it permits accessibility to everyone and is one of Russia's fastest-growing cities. This project aroused my interest in my assignment to Perm. By Russian standards I found it a very cosmopolitan place with many ethnic groups.

There are Russian Orthodox churches, mosques and synagogues and several Catholic churches, some dating back to 17th-century and existing next to each other. I attended Russian orthodox services with several of my Russian co-workers from the cheese plant. It starts at midnight and continued till noon. There are no pews and everyone must stand. I was amazed how many old ladies would stand, praying; celebrating the rise of Christ on Easter Sunday services. Needless to say one hour was the extent of devotional obligation at a Russian Orthodox Church.

The multicultural character of Perm also shows in architecture, countless little kiosks, theaters and trolley buses everywhere. This all makes Perm as Russian as Russia can be. Everywhere I went I was welcomed by my hosts. I would always carry a photo album of my family and my cheese factory. and they would enjoy looking at the album. Maybe next time bring your wife.

"Viva" Ltd. & "Trud" Ltd.
MILK PROCESSING TECHNOLOGIES
1. PROJECT INFORMATION
A. Project Number: HQ #: 331183   Field #: MAV127
B. Project Location: Country: Russia Oblast/Krai: Perm

HOST # 1
Name   Niva Ltd.Liability Co
Primary Contact Zomarev
   Dmitriyevich, Director
Address 617530 Russia Perm Aspa Village

Host #2
Name Trud Ltd Liability Co

   Primary Contact: Yushkov Yury Alexandrovich, Director
   Address: 617438 Russia, Perm oblast
                        Kungurskiy raion, Troelga village
   Organizational Plans/Goals:
1) Immediate
The immediate goals of Niva Ltd. are to improve the quality of the hard cheese currently produced and expand the assortment of hard and processed cheese.

The immediate goals of the Trud company are to improve the overall quality of the milk products and increase the products' shelf life.

III. Description of Volunteer Assignment "A". Problem Statement:

At the Niva company, their product assortment is quite common for any other dairy processing operation in Russia and consists of pasteurized milk, sour cream, curds, butter and one type of hard cheese. Obviously, it is very hard to compete on the market with such a limited product assortment.

Niva Ltd Komo Joint Stock Co

May 9, 2001
IVAN ZOMAREV DIRECTOR
PROJECT No 331183
TAMARA ZOMAREV DIRECTOR OF MILK PLANT   Host (1)

I have been invited to come to the Aspen village to review the current cheese manufacturing operations and evaluate the possibility of expanding into new varieties. Also, to help evaluate the present operations to see what improvements can be made. This is a cheese maker to cheese maker exchange of ideas to foster better relations with Russia in the agricultural industry.

The Niva plant is currently undergoing construction of a new barn and milk parlor for 250 milking cows. A German company, Westphalia, is providing equipment and the latest technology at the Niva farm. They expect to increase their annual herd milk yields with new feeds fortified with vitamin supplements. These new facilities should also eliminate problems with the quality of raw milk.

With increased milk production they need to become familiar with the technology of natural hard cheese, processed cheese and cheese spreads. Also, many new products can be made from sour cream, which is a staple in the Russian diet.

This is my fourteenth trip to Russia in this capacity.

Niva Plant Accomplishments - *part 2*

My first task was to introduce about twenty varieties of cheese and dairy products manufactured at Kutter's Cheese Factory.

The plant director and her staff tasted and evaluated the samples. We discussed and determined what types of cheese would lend itself to be made on the equipment available in the plant.

Cheddar cheese curd was chosen. Not only could it be sold immediately, it could be flavored with various dry seasonings such as onions, chives, garlic and pizza flavors. We produced several batches and it improved with each consecutive batch. Next we

133

turned our attention to processed cheese spreads. We were able to use the cheese they made. We devised a formula where we could use a blend of cheddar, tvorog, sour cream and cheese whey. I had all the necessery stabilizers and emulsifiers with me. All these are available on the Russian market now.

They could purchase undergrade cheese and use all the other types of cheese needed from their own production. This cheese has a high moisture content, making it highly profitable. It can be highly automated if produced in large quantities.

I detected some flavor defects, which I suspected to be from the milk supply. To overcome this we need to have a program to improve milk supply by selecting good milk. Our final results were satisfactory.

We were able to train laboratory staff on the new methods of testing for coli and pathogens in raw milk. I had brought with me all the materials that I needed to perform these tests.

Niva Plant Recommendation Part 3

It was with great pleasure that I had the opportunity to work so closely with everyone at the Niva Plant

Just an Added Suggestion

If this were my plant I would install a small ice cream freezer. Only for retail sales in the village. In the US there are small ice cream freezers available for in store sales. Wholesaling of ice cream would be too expensive. The equipment needed is to great an investment for a profitable return at this time. Children and families would make the cheese factory a focal point in the community, especially in the summer.

Trud Plant – Part 2

Recommendations are basicly the same as for the Niva plant
My recommendations

1) Begin a research program in the laboratory with the intent of manufacturing hard cheese and cheese spreads in the future When they perfect these products they can introduce them to the people of the village through their stores and see if there is customer acceptance.
2) While I was there our tests indicated a load of poor milk was accepted. A program is needed to follow up and resolve these problems
3) Discuss with engineer to fabricate some implements needed to start producing cheese curd and muenster.
4) Produce ice cream for the village residents. I may be able to assist in finding an American ice cream freezer at low cost.

5) There was an interest in my wastewater disposal system. I had a meeting with the sanitation inspectors. They took a great interest in our system from an ecology standpoint and low operating costs. It might be worth investigating this issue.

Summary Trud Plant

We were successful with our cheese making. We demonstrated the technology and methods of producing cheddar cheese curd, muenster, cheese spreads and a sweet Russian dessert cheese.

I had photos of our wastewater treatment facilities at my cheese factory in the United States. Yuri was very interested in our system. They asked the sanitary inspectors from the region to meet with me. They would like to adapt a similar system in their plant in the future. Before my departure from Trud Plant Yuri invited all the staff from the processing plant to his office. We all tasted the new cheese products we had produced. Irena spoke at length about the importance of entering into cheese production. She felt they had enough know how and background in the technology to proceed. We all felt that Yuri was very pleased and that he was convinced it was a good idea to further explore and experiment in cheese making. He wants to work out the economics and determine its profitability.

Again I would like to thank ACDI-VOCA and all the people at the Trud Plant for giving me the opportunity to share my knowledge and know how. Hopefully they will start producing cheese sometime in the future.

Omsk
"Moskalensky " Cheese Plant

B. Project Location: Country: Russia Oblast/Krai: Omsk oblast

Because of the completion of building a cheese plant in Omsk Russia I have been receiving numerous requests to return to Siberia. I have accepted this assignment at the Moskalensy Cheese Plant to try and improve their cheese production. After departing from the US and arriving in Moscow I had a briefing at the ACDI-VOCA office in Moscow and immediately departed to Siberia. Arriving in Omsk I was picked up by my host from the Moskalensky Cheese Plant. On completion of my assigment I left for Novosibirsk office, an affiliate of Land 0' lakes Inc, for debriefing. Mr. Slava Sundukov was our Russian, US in house director of operations in Siberia. I had a long chat with him about furthur assigments in Siberia.

Since the fall of communism Siberia has often been labeled the land of opportunity. If I look at the map of Canada and the US, Siberia reminds me of the 30 million people who live in Canada as it stretches along the border of the US. If you look at a map of Siberia most of the population stretches along the southern border of Siberia along the Trans Siberian Railway. Its climate is like Minnesota or Manitoba or even maybe Ontario Canada. I feel more at home in this part of Russia than I do in the Moscow region. I told Slava Sandukov I would be pleased to return and continue my work in Omsk and Novisibirsk region if time permits. Thank God for e-mail! It makes it is so easy to converse quickly and keep updated.

At present the host company has 180 employees. There are four cheese-vats on the plant with a capacity of ten metric tons each, but at present the plant does not use the cheese production equipment to its full capacity.

The host company buys two thirds of raw milk from about 10 farms, located nearby, and one third - from private individuals

Omsk Region/Oblast

I have made an effort to study the economics of this country where I have spent so much time. Again many economists say Siberia could be the lands of the future.

Novosibirst Oblast

Slava Sundukov, Novosibirsk Office Director Land O'Lakes, Inc. Novosibirsk Tel/fax: 7-3832-48-35-43; 7-3832-48-67-98. E-mail: slavalol(a@sibmail.ru Cell phone for emergency contacts: 8-913-910-60-21 - Slava Sundukov

Apr 25, 2005
Oblast/Krai: Omsk Oblast
Russia

Scope of work

At this plant they produce an albumen tvorog with a small market potential. They need to remove the solids from the whey so it is easier to dispose of the watery part of the milk as a waste product. In the US whey is dried and there are many uses for dried whey in the confectionary, bakery, and other food industries. The director has indicated to me that he wants to find a use for this product. I feel this product can be utilized.

Accomplishment

They were most interested in my processed cheese spreads and hard processed cheese with flavors. His main interest was to utilize his albumen tvorog in a processed cheese spread. He inquired if there was any chance to use up to 50% in my formulations. He then informed me that they had experimented with different formulas before and failed. They attempted to do this in the plant rather than set it up in a laboratory procedure where many variations in formulations could be experimented with. There are many chemical changes occurring when using different stabilizers and emulsifiers. Different stages of curing cheese cause different melting ability or creaming out as we refer to in the industry. I brought with me all the additional ingredients needed such as emulsifiers, stabilizers and seasonings for this formulation. There are many stabilizers that react chemically in various ways to gain the necessary texture and body when using different dairy products. This tvorog has only the whey proteins and milk sugars with a moisture content of 80%. We used my skim milk powder, some butter and brought the ratio of solid to fat more to its original balance in cheese. We tried many different formulations until we came up with a very satisfactory cheese spread. We were successful in using up to 50% of his tvorog in the cheese spread. Vladimir was very pleased with the results.

We made a tour of the facility to determine the type of equipment best suited for commercial production of this new product. Vladimir asked me if I would continue my assistance by attempting to secure some used machinery from the US. Upon my return I will contact some of my equipment dealers and keep in contact with the director of the Moskalensky plant. There was also much interest in hard processed cheese which we were also able to produce. Other cheeses that were of great interest were cheddar cheese curds and cream cheese. Unfortunately our time ran out. Hopefully we can continue our new product development at a later assignment.

Summary

I strongly urge the Moskalensky Cheese Plant to continue their R&D work to develop new varieties of cheese. Vladimir Sokolenko has a positive outlook for the future of his enterprise and its employees. He is aggressively seeking new product development to increase the profitability of the company.

I want to thank Vladimir Sokolensky and ACDI-VOCA for inviting me to the Moskalensky Cheese plant to share all my technology with him. I would also like to thank my interpreter Olesya Markimova for assisting me in my work. She has a Masters degree in agronomy and her knowledge of agriculture was very beneficial to my work. She was very competent in translating all my technological data. I hope I can be of further assistance to the Moskalensky cheese plant in the future.

Ichalkovskiy Cheese Production Plant
Feb 12, 2005
Nickoli Kireer, Director
Oblast/Krai Mordovia Republic
Russia RQ#:331544

Scope of assignment

I was invited by ACDI-VOCA, Moscow office, to develop new cheeses and dairy products at the Ichalkovskiy cheese facility in the Mordovia Republic.

They were especially interested in the latest technology from the US and how I operated my plant and marketed our products in America This plant was constructed in 1934. It was on the verge of bankruptcy after the break up of the Soviet Union. It has had over 20 directors since the collapse of communism.

Nickoi Kireer was hired to help turn the company around. He hired Elena Rubsova, chief technologist, to become production supervisor. With strong leadership and discipline they were able to steadily bring the company into the profit column and reduce the huge debts. The work staff was reduced and farmers are now paid for their milk on time. These facts are all chronicled in a book published about the history of the Ichalkovskiy Cheese Plant.

The Mordovia Republic is similar to Wisconsin where agriculture plays a very important role in the economy.

President Nichoi Merkuskin and the the Assembly gave a grant to Ichalkovskiy Cheese Plant to modernize with the most state of the art automated equipment from Spain. This plant is operating below capacity because of a milk deficit. The director informed me they could market more product than currently producing. We are now making cheese with my technology in Samara, Uglish, Alti Republic and a plant near Omsk.

The Ichalkovskiy Cheese Plant is located in the village Ichalki, Ichalkovskiy, an area of Mordovia. It was founded in 1934 and is one of the biggest cheese plants in Mordovia. The plant is mainly involved in hard and processed cheese production. Besides this, plant produces butter, pack milk and some sour milk products (cottage cheese, ryazhenka and bifidok).

The company's main products include twenty six cheese varieties including hard and soft rennet cheeses and processed cheese.

A year ago the company bought a Spanish technological line with fully automatic equipment for hard cheese production which consists of 2 cheese producers (closed kettles with 10 tons capacity each), 1 molding machine, 2 tunnel presses, Ihorizontal press, a machine for removing caps from cheese molders

Sweet cottage cheese with raisins and dried apricots is packed in foil and plastic containers, while sour milk beverages are packed in polyethylene packages. In future, the company is planning to buy a Tetra Pack or Techno Pack packaging line.

Raw milk suppliers are located in Mordovia Republic and in the neighboring republics.

Currently, many of the food processing enterprises in Russia experience the same types of problems as any other agricultural enterprise in Russia. A lack of updated and modern technologiy, limited product assortment, lack of expertise and knowledge, and a lack of funds.

I was told one of the buyers of Ichalkovsiky cheese products inquired about American style cottage cheese. I have visited many Russian cheese plants. There always was a favorable response to this product. I recommended introducing this product into the market.

Alterative non-dairy fat such as vegetable oil to reduce aterial cost have been used in Russia. This also occurred in the US but was a failure due to lack of taste. I would discourage it. Consumers want the taste of real cheese.

Keep up the good work. This organization has what it takes to grow and become an icon in the Russian cheese industry.

The Gulag Museum in Perm Russia

It was December 1987 that this Gulag finally closed its doors. All other camps were destroyed, but a coalition of former inmates, human rights activists, and Russian historians were able to save this camp. When I was in Perm it had not yet been open to the public. When I was on assignment in Perm it was not something that was openly discussed and I always felt that if they were not responsive I certainly would not pursue my discussion or my interest. Most generally my colleagues would say it is just part of our history.

Omsk State University

Recruitment note: We recommend Tony Kutter as a suitable candidate for this assignment.

FARMER-TO-FARMER CONSORTIUM
Scope of Work
OMSK STATE AGRICULTURAL UNIVERSITY
"TYUKALINSKI "CHEESE PLANT
   Natalia Gavrilova, Vice-Rector of the Omsk State Agricultural University for Innovations, used to be the head of this Chair. She learned about Farmer to Farmer program from her colleagues from other Departments of Omsk Ag. University and applied for technical assistance in improvement of the dairy processing/cheese making curriculum.

REQUESTING ORGANIZATION
A. HOST #1

Name: Omsk Agricultural University

Primary Contact: Gavrilova Natalia Borisovna.,
Deputy Rector of Innovations
Secondary Contact: Maksimova Oleysya, Assistant for
                                   the Vice-rector for Foreign Affairs

HOST #2
Name: "Tyukalinski" Cheese Plant
Primary Contact: Konovalov Ivan Petrovich, Cheese
Plant Director

Secondary Contact: Gavrilova N. B., Deputy Rector on Innovations of Omsk State Agricultural Universtiy

After completing construction of a cheese plant and training Russians to operate and manufacture cheese at Neudochio plant I made numerous return trips to work in the Omsk Oblast. I would travel with Olesya Marsimova, acting as my translator. She was a graduate of Omsk Agricultural State University, now working toward her PhD in agronomy. It was a pleasure working with her and she was very enthusiastic about learning cheese production and dairy bacteriology.

I received an e-mail from Olesya asking if I would consider conducting a seminar at her university. I wrote back and asked her what would she like me to present to her students. She selected a few topics that would be interesting to students studying food science, especially cheese making. They had all the necessary equipment to present power point programs.

This was a challenge for me. I have some basic knowledge of working on the computer but lecturing at a university and making my own lesson plans is something I haven't done. I have to tip my hat and thank my daughter-in-law June Kutter who is in charge of quality control in the laboratories at Kutters Cheese Factory. She helped me develop programs and download them on a CD. I also called upon many of my suppliers of cultures, rennet and professors at Cornell University who advised me on numerous topics and programs that they use for their undergrad students.

April 8-9-10

I arrived in Moscow and stayed at the Bega Hotel. The next morning I was picked up by the driver and taken to the ACDI-VOCA office for briefing then left that evening on Siberian Airlines for Omsk.

April 11-12

I arrived in Omsk 5 AM, was picked up by Olesya Maksimova and her father. They took me to the Molodyoznhanya Hotel. The next morning he picked me up and we went to the University where I met Natalie Gavrilova.

April 13-14 and 15th

I put on my first power point program about Kutters Cheese Factory from 1947 to 2007, also a program on robotic milking of cows. We now have some farms in the US where cows are milked by robots. There is absolutely nobody in the milking parlor. It truly is an incredible thing to see in operation. Everyone was fascinated with it. This engineering marvel hasn't arrived in Russia yet.

I carried with me 20 varieties of cheese and described in detail the characteristics of each cheese and everyone tasted it and we recorded the type of cheese, its pH value, moisture content and characteristic flavor.

We had a power point program presentation on the fundamentals of cheese making.

a) component parts of milk
b) Cultures
c) Rennet and enzymes
d) Various types of cheese and the curing of cheese
e) Surface cured cheese and mold varieties such as camembert and blue cheese.

The laboratory at the university had some very basic cheese making equipment. We made our first batch of cheddar cheese starting with pasteurized milk with our cultures and rennet. We followed the step-by-step presentation in my power point program, the fundamentals of cheese making. We completed the project with two small wheels of cheddar cheese and we went on to make other varieties of cheese. The students were very interested and had never seen milk made into cheese. I had brought along some laboratory supplies to enable us to perform coliform test on our product to ensure the cleanliness and wholesomeness of our cheese. We also did analysis on the milk. The next lecture was on how to make clean milk, good sanitation on the farm and the importance of good quality milk and cheese production. A second program was presented about my 12 years and 30 trips to Russia building cheese factories and training Russians in new product development.

Host No 2

When I travelled toTyukalinski cheese plant I was met by Director Ivan Konovalov. The plant had old equipment from the Soviet period although it had been maintained quite well. Cheese consisted mostly of Russian and Dutch varieties. They were mostly interested in how we operate our cheese factory in the US. I also presented a short program on robotic milking where there are absolutely no people milking cows. These robotic machines have been proven successful. If they malfunction the farmer automatically receives a call on his cell phone. If he's in the field with his tractor he returns to the milk house, adjusts the robotic electronics to working order and returns to the field.

They are considering increasing their product line. Next I demonstrated a few of the products we produce in the US. Will these products appeal to their customer base, would enough milk be available? I proposed a cheddar cheese curd that can be sold immediately and have a long shelf life.

There was no new decision made about producing new products however they want to increase production in the future. I am not sure what they actually propose to do.

It was Sunday and my work had been completed at the University. Olesya, Natalie and her husband drove us to a place that was formerly a prison (Gulag). After perestroika an Orthodox church was built there. They told me that there were some new Russian rich people who built small chapels for their families who could pray there. I felt it was more for gaining recognition. There also was a spa where warm water came out of the ground warm enough to swim in even in the winter. Afterwards we went to a history museum and had dinner at a hotel. The following day we visited a modern state of the art ice cream plant called Enmarke, highly automated plant with equipment from Denmark. I surmise this was an example of Russians Oligarchs who are now investing their money in Russia. It is becoming difficult for a small businessman in today's Russia. The trend will continue to have fewer and larger plants.

It was a sad farewell after completing a very successful program conducting a seminar in a Russian University, something that was a little bit out of my element but a wonderful diversion. Olesya's father gave me some Russian souvenirs which I really treasured. It was a huge banner of Lenin and the Komsomol with various pins attached that young Russians receive as they grew up in this organization under communism. It is like our Boy Scouts and you would earn merit badges and hopefully end up as an Eagle Scout in good standing in the community. Her father said he would like a polo shirt with an American flag. I sent him one in the mail and it never arrived. On a later trip I returned to Omsk and met up with Olesya and her father and I presented a shirt that I carried with me. This was the second time I sent gifts that never arrived. All my Russian colleagues told me not to send it by mail. We will never receive it. It's hard to fathom that sending something in our US Postal Service would not arrive. They took me to the Omsk airport and I caught a flight back to Moscow, was debriefed and flew back home.

I now have this banner with Lenin hanging in my cheese and wine tasting gallery at our cheese plant. Olesya's father told me many Russians are collecting old communist memorabilia today. I am very fortunate to have this as a souvenir.

Young Pioneers and the Konsomol

Occasionally someone will ask what does that banner say in Russian. It reads:

> "The Konsomol is a Union of Communist youth who must be forever cognizant and strong and show great initiative and help in promoting a socialistic society with honor.

So often people who were absorbed in their wine tasting just say what is that all about. I would ask, when you were young were you into scouting? Did you earn merit badges? Invariably most people spent part of their youth in scouting. I have a son Tom and grandson James who attained the rank of Eagle Scout that made me proud. This is an admirable trait, especially when it's on your resume applying at a university or job. However, about only 2% of our Boy Scouts remain dedicated long enough in the organization to attain the rank of Eagle Scout.

In Russia, the Young Pioneers is similar to our scouts only more so. They all had uniforms symbolic of the Young Pioneers with red banners, a flag, red tie and a badge of Vladimir Lenin. The inscription read "Always Ready".

On many occasions while working in Russia I was invited to dinner by my fellow workers. We had such stimulating conversation exchanging thoughtful reflections about our own lives from the time we went to school, selecting a university, getting married, raising a family and pursuing our jobs or professions.

FARMER TO FARMER CONSORTIUM

Primary contact: Director	Alyp L Ltd Kardamanov Sergey Ivanovich,
Address:	649100 Gorno-Altai Republic, Maima Village, Nagornaya 1
Host No2: Company	"Maimi Moloko" Ltd Cherga Cheese Making
Address:	Aefay Rep Cherga Director Egor Serov

Alyp Ltd is located in Maima village, approximately 5 km from Gorno-Altaisk. "Aicon" company is mainly involved in cheese production and is located in Maima village. The Butter-Cheese Plant was founded in 1977 as a state dairy processing enterprise, and in 1994 it was reorganized into a Limited liability company. The company's main products include:

- processed/melted cheese(Ohotnik, Omichka, Yantar, Shokoladny);
- rennet cheese (Yglichesky, Kostromskoy);
- non-fat cheese (Pletenka, Gorodskoi); and
- soybean cheese spread (Tofu).

In addition, the host produces a Russian version of cottage cheese and powder milk.

All of the equipment is domestically made and quite old. Equipment consists of the following pieces: four vats; one homogenizing machine; two smoking chambers; three automated packaging machines; and one vacuum sealer.
eration and increase their cheese product assortment.

At present, the company is adopting "know-how" technologies of hard cheeses production ("Hero", "Russian", "Dutch"), and production of classic milk butter. The company can process up to 70 tons of milk per day. The good quality of the local raw milk gives the company an opportunity to produce higher quality cheeses. In the nearest future it is planned to adopt the production technologies for classical "swiss" and "soviet" cheeses.

The management of the enterprise would like to invite an Farmer to Farmer volunteer to help improve the cheese processing operation and increase their cheese product assortment.

Altai Republic Russia

PROJECT NUMBER HQ #;LOL 100
OBLAST/KRAI GORNO-ALTI
APR 2003

This region of of Russia was one of the most unique trips I have made. It reminded me of Switzerland with mountains, lakes and streams without all the people. It was the first cheese plant in Russia where I would be making swiss cheese. As we traveled these long highways across the mountains in a Russian jeep I could see farmers on horseback herding cattle. These cows roamed the mountains freely, a perfect environment for dairy cows. My thoughts turn to my childhood when I loved to watch western cowboy movies. These cowboys on horseback had Mongolian features somewhat like our American Indians.

Swiss cheese is considered the "King of Cheese" one of the most

difficult cheeses to make and maintain consistency. It requires very low amounts of culture, most of which is prevalent in the milk that's suitable for making cheese with beautiful eyes (holes). I have found that in many modern cheese factories in America where cows are fed corn silage there are thermordoric bacteria (bacteria that survive pasteurization) in corn silage It gets into the milk and causes problems, blowing up, cracks and improper gas development. This interferes with the development of the eyes, causing cheese of inferior quality. In Switzerland corn silage is not allowed. In the Altai region corn does not grow in this climate. Cows generally graze on grass and consume suitable rations.

One never realizes all the mysterious places that exist in Russia. The Altai Republic and its remoteness left a memorable impression. This land still keeps the traces of an ancient civilization. It is located in southwest Russia along the border of Mongolia, China and Kazakhstan. The Altai is considered to be the crossroads to the ancient world to people of this region. The people of the Altai welcomed foreign visitors with friendliness and warmth. For me it was an unforgettable experience.

June 3, 2003

I arrived in Moscow after a long flight from Buffalo to Atlanta to New York to Moscow. Then it's a two-hour drive from the Moscow airport to downtown Moscow to the Aerostar Hotel. I finally arrived at 4 PM. I set down my suitcase, refrigerated cheese samples and materials and crashed onto the bed. I took a long nap then that evening I went out and bought some hot food and a few bottles of beer went back to my hotel and had supper. I just don't like to eat in a restaurant by myself. The next morning I went to the office for briefing, everybody in the office welcomed my return. Michael Harvey wanted me to give them a brief synopsis of my years of involvement with the Russian cheese industry to use for his annual report to Washington. I left for Moscow's Domededowo airport for a flight to Novosibirsk, Siberia. This is like flying from New York to San Francisco. I was picked up by a driver assigned to me and he drove me to a hotel "SIBIR" on the river Ob. It was another long day but I always slept well and was rested up for the next day. My driver picked me up and took me to the Land O Lakes Inc. where I met Director Slava Sundokov for further briefing. The plan was that I was to travel by bus 400 miles to Gorno - Alaisk to Host #1. After that assignment I would go to host# 2 and would travel to Barnul. I was to meet my translator Mr. Aidir Koudirmekov in the morning who would meet me at the hotel. He would be traveling with me during my time in the Altai Republic.

This guy was so eccentric and he was late picking me up. He had Mongolian features and dressed in casual shorts and sandals. I just assumed we would walk over to the bus station and catch a bus to Gorno-Alaisk as it was specifically spelled out in assignment. He just took the portfolio with specific information about my assignment and tossed it in his car. He had his own plans. He drove up in a car that was a piece of junk and we had to drive 400 miles to our destination on a very warm day. He said we're not riding in a bus 400 miles. I was quite concerned about the deviation and his complete take-over of our whole itinerary. All these agencies are very strict and concerned about our safety and welfare. If serious problems occurred they are held responsible. This would blemish and tarnish the future of our Farmer To Farmer program. He said, "No problem we will drive ourselves and I will just charge you for the gas, it will be less than two bus tickets" He was carrying several 5 gallon cans of water. He told me he had a little problem with a radiator, a slow leak. By the evidence of the water on the ground I thought to myself this is a serious problem and it was a very hot day in June. We constantly stopped at gas stations to fill up the radiator and water cans. The problem was there weren't many gas stations and we had to keep going till we found water somewhere in these mountains. After about 300 miles the car overheated so badly the engine just seized up. He literally cooked the motor. We were in the mountains and it was getting dark. He walked a ways and located someone who he negotiated a price of $50 to tow the car, while I sat in the car near the Mongolian border. He had a friend who had a little hut on top of a mountain were he towed it to. He handed me a hand full of gasoline receipts and the $50 towing bill for reimbursement. I thought to myself how I am going to explain this in my expense report. It certainly was not allowed. He said, "I will keep track of your expenses and you will be reimbursed by Land O Lakes". I just didn't know how this was going to play out but I had never been in a situation like this. This little place on top of the mountain was a broken down shamble. Now it was very late into the night. I slept on a bed where I don't think the sheets have been changed in years. Adair slept in a dirty sleeping bag on the ground floor. Somehow I found this somewhat hilarious. I certainly was in no danger out here in the wilderness amongst little hamlets were farmers lived. These people are very warm and friendly. They spoke their own language and Adair could speak it also. There are hundreds of languages and dialects spoken in this vast land.

I took pictures of the surroundings and the conditions of this mountain hut where I stayed to be able to show my friends about my adventures. Adair took my film and said there was a two hour photo shop in the city and he would take them there and pick them up for me. When I looked at them I noticed the pictures of this dirty hut and car were not amongst them but they were in my negatives. He deliberately had taken pictures he did not want me to show anyone. I did not confront him about it because I still had my whole assignment ahead of me. He was always trying to make my assignment more enjoyable and he loved to go out after work and have a drink and look for young women. I always got the impression that he was so happy to be assigned to an American and use his English language skills. He had never done this before. He was a very interesting person and I met some of his family. I never thought in my wildest dream I would be making cheese in this part of the world. I still haven't met anyone in America that has heard of the Altai republic. The next morning a relative of his took us the nearest village to catch a bus rest of the way to the cheese plant.

I was finally able to put my cheese samples under refrigeration. I had everything packed in ice packs in Styrofoam containers but it was very warm day in June. This didn't help the quality of my cheese. The cheese plant had a driver who took us to a lodge like a bed and breakfast in the mountains. It was a very beautiful place. Adair had relatives nearby whom he stayed with. I took a shower and got a good night's rest.

The following morning I met the director and owner of Alyps cheese plant, Sergey Kardmanov and chief technologist Tatiana

Leoniova, They were making mozzarella and processed cheese. They had purchased the information from Nickoli Sheridan from Uglish whom I had trained in making Italian American style mozzarella. I mentioned to Sergey about my work in Uglish and he seemed to be aware that I had worked with Nickoli. They wanted to make cheddar cheese and cheddar cheese curd. He was quite impressed with the different varieties of processed cheese that I had carried with me to present to him. We did a tour of his plant to examine some of the equipment that would be available to make experimental cheese. It was late Friday afternoon so we went out for dinner and I returned to my lodge in the mountains. We planned on making some cheese on Monday. I decided it was going to be a good chance for me to relax, do some writing, put together my reports and just kind of walk around the area and chat with people who were staying in the lodge. Most of the guests vacationing here were river rafting in nearby streams. It was a warm day, and everybody was out with their rafts in the turbulent waters rafting down the river. Sergey and Tatiana said to me when they dropped me off we may be here tomorrow morning and will give you a tour of the area. Little did I know about their plan.

Saturday, June 9, 2003 -- Sunday, June 10

I had a breakfast with Russian pancakes and kiefer with cheese and sausage and coffee. I just settled down to write up some of my reports and a daily log when Sergey and Tatiana pulled up in a Russian jeep. They informed me that we were leaving right now for an overnight camping trip in the mountains. I said I'm not prepared to go on overnight camping trip, I have no equipment. He said we took care of that, he had a sleeping bag and a pup tent for me. He had vodka, wine, steaks, potatoes, salads and everything was prepared. He took fire wood, cooking gear and said let's go. I put my papers away, grabbed some clothes and jumped in the Jeep and we started out. We drove several hundred miles into the mountains heading to one of the most desolate place where there was a beautiful lake in the middle of the mountains. He said I haven't been here in years, I hope I can find it. I always wanted to come back and now I want to show you our Altai region. We had a hard time finding it, it was a little off the road and the mountain trail had been completely grown over with trees. When we located it he pulled off the road, put the jeep and four-wheel drive and we all hung on as we traversed over some pretty rough terrain. The last mile we failed to complete because of overgrown fallen trees. We set up our camp and walked back to the lake. It was crystal-clear water surrounded by beautiful forests, a beautiful setting. It was quite warm so we all went swimming. We returned to our camp and started a fire. He had all the necessary equipment and lots of food. We toasted our friendship with vodka and cognac while the steaks and potatoes were cooking. Tatiana whipped up a salad. He had a warm sleeping bag, air mattresses and a tent for me. I have never had so much to eat. I slept soundly and that night I could hear cuckoos all night. I have a cuckoo clock at home. I asked is that a cuckoo bird I keep hearing. Yes, just like in Switzerland or the Bavarian Mountains. In the morning we had breakfast again with steak, potatoes and leftovers. We packed up and started home. We stopped at a restaurant and had lunch. I bought some souvenir books of the Altair Republic region. We went back to my lodge. It was a great weekend and we were all very tired following the long ride back. There's an old proverb in Russia when western foreigners say you should have more freedom (meaning political freedoms). If you want freedom go out into the forests and enjoy the freedom. The Siberians love to do this after the cold winters. It can get very hot during their short summers. These occasions were so memorable

Monday morning we arrived at the plant and they had some milk ready for us. We made some cheese curd and it turned out the best I have ever made in Russia. We flavored it with different flavorings and I felt so good about it. We also did some tests for coli and some tests on the quality of milk and milk was of good quality. Next day we returned to the plant and packaged the cheese. We had a discussion about regional markets for cheese. They had a very good reputation here at this plant and they had markets in some other cities in the Altair Republic. They were interested in processed cheese and cheese spread. They didn't have the machinery to manufacture it commercially, but we did produce sample batches in their laboratory so they could monitor and record makes procedures for future consideration. I informed them about a Russian company that manufactures cheese processing equipment whom I have met with. This company invited me to meet with them and asked if I would promote their equipment. They have quality equipment at half the cost of European fabricators.

Next, Adair and I traveled to the Cherga plant where they make Swiss cheese. As usual he was late. He was quite a drinker and womanizer and love to party. We did go out the previous evening had a nice meal and I think he consumed too much alcohol. When we arrived at the plant I could tell he was really feeling bent over. I told him I didn't think I needed him as a translator and they found a place for him to get a little rest and he slept most of the day. I met with Elena Logvinova, chief technologist; she wasn't getting the proper eye development (holes in swiss cheese). I brought with me cultures to utilize for Swiss cheese. Swiss cheese is heated to a very high temperature and they were using cultures that were more suited for cheese like edam or gouda. I had with me some burglarious, thermophilous and propionic bacteria needed for swiss cheese production It takes six weeks to cure swiss and develop proper eye formation. I was later told this did improve the quality and consistency of their cheese.

I wanted to spend more time at the Cherga cheese plant because it was the first time I was in the region for producing high-quality swiss cheese. We have been making swiss cheese in our US plant for over 40 years. Making swiss cheese is very challenging and I wanted to contribute as much knowledge and information as possible in the time allowed.

Aidar Koudirmekov, my translator, had other plans for me. We had made an exceptional batch of cheddar cheese curds with various flavors at Alyp Ltd cheese plant. Aidar said," today we are going to take a bus to the Altai-West Resort and we will take our cheese curd samples and present them on a sales call. Evidently he had been in contact with them in regards to employment as a translator for foreign guests. This was not on my agenda so I was concerned and uneasy if there were any deviation from our itinerary. Aidar assured me he had everything under control and he knew these people personally and they would be very anxious to see our product. We'll just call it hosts number 3. He didn't see any problem with Land O' Lakes when I filled out my report. He seemed to feel he was in charge and Slava Sundokov, our director, at Land O' Lakes would certainly approve. We caught a bus and traveled to the Belokuricha region of the Altai and arrived at this beautiful resort in the mountains. There was also a ski resort and year-round complex for entertainment and a sanatorium. The first thing they did when I arrived they gave me a short physical, asked if I had any ailments or pains. They took my blood pressure, it was borderline so they told me to take a nice long rest and gave me some blood pressure medication. Of course I felt somewhat stressed-out which would invariable cause one's blood pressure to rise. I had this occur when I was building cheese plant in Neudochino. I remember they always checked the truck drivers when they arrived to check for sobriety and blood pressure. The nurses said border line is not a problem to them; it's when it's way off the chart.

Altai West Resort

The Velvet of Deer Antlers

My time spent in this sanatorium was an educational and learning experience for me. Altai West was highly recognized for medicinal products made from deer antlers. I have to admire how under the socialism retirees enjoyed the health benefits of these resorts. This is often a part in European and Asian cultures. I always remember my mother's nostalgia about how she could go to a sanatorium in the Black Forest and enjoy all the therapeutic attention and pampering. It just made one forget about all the aches and pains prevalent with aging. It was even paid for by their socialized free medical insurance. My mother said it just does not exist here in the United States.

They gave me a gift of deer antler velvet powder extract. I was 70 years old at the time and everybody said you are in good health and you must take this to sustain yourself for continued good health. This was an intriguing gift and I was engrossed in all aspects of this medicinal medication. Would this really make me a new man again? The staff here said you will be pleasantly surprised. Anyway it does arouse ones spirits when you are in a remote part of the world where everything interests you.

History

Deer antler velvet has a very fascinating history. It is a medicinal extraction from large deer horns. Velvet from deer antlers has been used for thousands of years. There is evidence of velvet documented on the Chinese ancient scrolls back to 100 BC.

According to tradition it creates increased blood flow within the body which contributes to more energy. It is a traditional Chinese medicine and available throughout the world including the US.

I met with the director, Jury Lidzhievich of Altai-West Resort. They received guests from all over the world but never from America. I never met any English-speaking guests at this complex. His desire was to have a cosmopolitan cuisine and he was interested in the cheese curd and mozzarella. After tasting the samples we made at the Alyp plant he immediately placed an order. I said, "We could not provide this cheese until we purchased proper equipment to make it. I also had discussed how at my cheese plant how we combined a winery and a cheese factory in the same facility. Our goal was to promote two great agricultural products, wine and cheese. I told him how we would have buses come to our cheese plant for wine and cheese tastings. Every one usually bought their favorite wine and some cheese. We discussed that every community had a chamber of commerce to promote tourism. This concept of bringing tourists to your cheese and wine gallery intrigued him and he was always looking for a way to entertain his guests. We had a discussion about the future of tourism in Russia and he said that so much was lost after the collapse of communism. We had so much to offer even our cheese technology was lost under Stalin's times. Hopefully, Russia will develop a larger society of upper middle class with financial means that can afford to spend vacations at our resort. Under the old communist system everyone retired at age 62 years and could go to resorts where sanatoriums are free. It was totally subsidized by the government. It is such a difficult transition for ordinary Russians. We lost so much, that's why many people have a great nostalgia for former days.

It was a very expensive place to stay but there are many Russians now that can afford it and are free to travel. Adair wanted to stay at this resort for the weekend and he negotiated a price with a 50% discount. I was even more disturbed and uneasy about my final expense report; if it was not authorized then I would be held accountable. I always carried extra money for my personal expenses. Credit cards were not accepted in this part of Russia as of yet. I was here to work with the Russian cheese industry not to entertain myself like a vacationer.

They gave us a suite with two bedrooms, living room and kitchen with all the latest kitchen necessities. What I was totally unaware of that he had arranged for two young ladies to spend the evening with us. There was a knock on the door. He'd answered the door and welcomed them and told me they had some wine and various snacks for us, Adair said, "They worked in the kitchen and felt obligated to entertain us. I was convinced they were prostitutes who were employed at this resort for more than one specific duty. Apparently Adair knew them personally. They poured us some wine and prepared some delicious snacks. We chatted with them, they were charming and I could chat with them in Russian. But they never seem anxious to leave. Finally I realized why they were here and I tried gracefully to just tell him that their services were no longer needed. However, Adair was not going to pass this up so finally he retired with the two ladies and I went off to bed myself.

Before we left on a bus back to Barnul he had a meeting with the director Jury Lidzhievich, paid the bill and had a discussion about his future employment opportunity at Altai West Resort. I never found out if he ever got the job. When we got back he handed me all the expenses he incurred and I paid them out of my stipend. I paid him for his translation service and gave him my hand held electronic translator as a gift which he was very happy to receive. It was a pleasure to work with him. One must remember this is another part of the world with different cultures and we don't want to be too critical. We parted and that's the last I ever heard from him. When I returned to Land O' Lakes office and had a very frank discussion about Adair. Slava expressed his concern. But he felt I had completed my assignment. I am sure Adair never received another opportunity to work with the Farmer to Farmer program with Citizens Network.

Altai Republic

The Altai Republic is situated in the very center of Asia at the junction of Siberian taiga, steppes of Kazakhstan and semi-deserts of Mongolia. The Altai Republic is the territory of highlands with a very picturesque landscape, a kind of "Russian Tibet" in the center of Eurasia at the junction of several states, natural zones and cultural worlds.

The Altai Republic borders on such remote countries as China and Mongolia and on near foreign country- Kazakhstan, which is the State border of the Russian Federation.

SUMMARY
I was very pleased with the response we received at the Altai West hotel and health center. They want to purchase 2000 lbs. of cheese, a tribute to all of us. Alyps Ltd. Cheese Co. who has a dedicated staff that work hard to produce quality cheese

I would like to thank Land O' Lakes and everyone who made it possible for me to participate in the farmer-to-farmer exchange. It was a great experience for everyone. I will continue to do everything I can to assist the Alyps Ltd Company and the Cherga Cheese Factory.
Tony Kutter

The Republic of Georgia

I received a call from ACDI-VOCA in Washington DC if I would return to the former Soviet Union and traveled to the Georgian Republic. I have often heard about the beauty of this country located on the Black Sea with the Caucasus Mountains rising in the background. When I was working in Russia I was just within a few miles of the border but was not allowed to enter the country.

I flew to Tbilisi, the capital of Georgia. It is a beautiful city located on the side the Caucasus Mountains. The name is derived from the old Georgian word meaning warm, also from the warm sulfuric hot springs coming out of the mountain sides. It is a city of lights and its distinguished balconies of various colors in the old part of the city. There is an effort to try to retain as much of the historic architecture as possible.

Ever since the breakup of the Soviet Union, Tbilisi experienced instability and turmoil. The Republic of Georgia is also the birthplace of Joseph Stalin and I truly wanted to visit his hometown before I completed this assignment.

Arriving at the Tbilisi airport from Vienna I was picked up by my driver, Gocha Mchedlishvili who spoke excellent English, and was taken to the Hotel "Kartli". This hotel was run by a German couple so I was able to converse with them in German. The following morning I was picked up by my driver and taken to ACDIVOCA Georgia office. I met with my Project director Magda Menadbe and project coordinator Nino Chanyuria. I was briefed and we had a long discussion about how the country and president Mikheil Saakashvili wanted to move his sphere of influence to the west into NATO. I was very surprised about their language. I just assumed that everyone spoke Russian. They have one of the oldest languages in the world and do not use the Cyrillic alphabet. The writing appears to look more like Arabic.

In my briefing they urged me not to speak Russian in public. They would prefer that I speak English and they would translate it for me and everyone would greet me with warm welcomes. One of the first things I noticed was all the street signs in huge letters were written in Georgian and underneath in English. I have never seen this in any part of the Soviet Union. In fact I had a polo shirt with an insignia "I love Russia". One morning when I had this shirt on my driver, Gocha Mchedlishvili said "please remove that shirt; I am not traveling with you wearing that shirt". The political relationships had cooled and the rhetoric had been become more confrontational. The Russians were boycotting all Georgian wine sales into Russia and even tropical fruit products were banned. They claimed the wine and fruit were contaminated. Georgian wine was always a favorite in Russia and aging wine will not contaminate itself. I still buy imported Georgian wine here in America just for the sake of nostalgia to commemorate my time spent working in the republic of Georgia.

After a thorough briefing about my assignment about Georgia, I retired to my hotel. The next morning Gotcha, my driver, picked me up and we drove several hundred kilometers to Teklati village of Samegrelo Region to meet with the director of "Nakoru" Ltd Cheese Factory and met Kakha Alania the director of cheese and farm operations. It was the only cheese factory in the region. He informed me under the Soviet system there were many collective farms and several milk processing facilities. However, many are now bankrupt or closed because of the loss of huge state subsidies provided for farms that no longer are available.

When I arrived at the cheese facility it was directly connected to the farm and appeared to be well constructed and clean. I was very pleased with this assignment because I had access to both the milk supply and the cheese factory. I felt that I could have a handle on quality control from the raw material to the finished product.

I was elated to receive this request to fulfill this assignment when they informed me this was the only cheese factory in Georgia. It had tremendous potential and I felt we could leave a mark upon completing this venture. You can't beat a good piece of cheese and a glass of splendid Georgian wine. Georgia was always a prosperous republic with its thriving agriculture and it warm tropical climate.

The Georgian people have paid an enormous price for their freedom from the former Soviet Empire.

Host is requesting Anthony Kutter for this assignment.
I. PROJECT INFORMATION

The Company's plans are to improve hard cheese production quality. They are looking at an expansion of the production and diversification of the products offered
The volunteer will be expected to:
  • Provide technology and recipe on hard (gauda, matsarela) cheeses production;
  • Provide information about shelf • Observe and evaluate

existing technological processes and factory equipment
used in cheese production;
- • Do the cost analyses of hard cheese production to see the
effectiveness and competitiveness of this business;
- •• Provide cultures for cheeses and make cheese at plant
while on assignment

C. Assignment Background

Senaki Dairy Company is company that consists of dairy cattle
farm and a milk processing plant. The 800 liters of raw milk is
processed on a daily basis for sour cream, cottage cheese, matsoni
and very small quantity of gauda cheese. Equipment allows the
company to process approximately 5 tons of raw milk per day. The
local production of milk is not sufficient in order to fully utilize the
capacity of equipment. The company management thinks of
collecting milk from neighboring villages by setting up mobile
collection stations.

With the current production the company is able to satisfy just a
small part of the existing demand for dairy products in west Georgia.

Political and Economic Situation

Georgia joined the USSR in 1922, continuing as the Georgian
Soviet Socialists Republic until 1990. Georgia was one of the first
republics of the Former Soviet Union (FSU) to declare
independence. This took place on April 9,

Georgia's economy has traditionally revolved around tourism,
cultivation of citrus fruits, tea, grapes, industrial and mining sectors,
and output of industrial sectors producing wine, metals, machinery,
chemicals and textiles. The country imports the bulk of its energy
needs, including natural gas and oil products. Its only sizable internal
energy resource is hydropower.

Agriculture

Agriculture is one of the most important sectors in the Georgian
economy. Approximately 50 percent of the population is engaged, to
some degree, in agriculture.

Because of its agricultural diversity and high export income,
Georgia became a major center of agricultural research and higher
education in the Soviet Union. The result is a highly educated work
force in a predominantly rural, but densely populated country.

'Nakoru' Ltd, Senaki Dairy Company

Senaki Rayon, Georgia

I demonstrated all my products to the director and chief
technologist, Zvidi. The owner Kaknar Alania decided to make gouda
cheese with my cultures. We discussed procedure which was similar

to our US gouda. The difference between ours and the Nakoru brands is that they had a very open texture. Our American gouda has a tight curd formation typical of the Holland's gouda, with occasional small holes the size of a pea, with a texture like swiss cheese.

The next day we produced cheddar cheese curd and introduced flavors in the product such as garlic, onion, dill and hot peppers. We were very successful and we packaged the cheese curd in 200 gram pouches which I also carried with me. They were very interested in this cheese curd because it has a financial advantage. It can be produced one day and sold the next. Gouda has to be aged for at least 60 days to develop its own characteristic flavor. They were selling their gouda cheese in 30 days and it just hadn't developed its optimum flavor. Aging cheese can tie up huge inventories and create a cash flow problem. A cash-strapped enterprise will not be able to sustain itself financially.

Next we use my culture to make Russian tvorog (a Russian farmer's cheese). We developed enough lactic acid in five hours compared to 14 hours with Russian cultures. Proper acid development is crucial when manufacturing any type of cheese. We also made American-style creamed cottage cheese. I also carried with me lab supplies to conduct various analytic tests on milk and final cheese products. It was a pleasure working in this plant because I could advise them how to produce good clean low bacteria milk from the farm that was adjacent to the cheese plant. The chief technologist had never seen the simple lab tests that have been developed here in America.

Kakhar Alania discussed with me his future interest in producing high-priced quality cheese such as blue cheese, swiss cheese and processed cheese. They did not have any of the equipment and curing facilities available to manufacture these types of cheeses. These imported cheeses are available in stores in cities like Tbilisi Georgia. He said, "There is now a clientele that is financially inclined to purchase these types of cheese". We would like to be the first and only cheese plant in all of Georgia producing this type of cheese.

With my cultures we made sour cream and we formulated recipes for salad dressings in chip dips. This was something entirely new to them. We conducted a final meeting with Kakhar Alania and his staff. We discussed all my recommendations for the farm and cheese plant.

1) Continue making cheese curd with various flavors. It appears it has consumer acceptance.
2) Make gouda cheese with these new cultures which will help guide proper development and flavor enhancement.
3) Consider swiss cheese, blue cheese and camembert possibilities for the future. I will return to continue with this technology and turn our attention to broaden their product

lines. Increase the size of herds on the farm and inquire from ACDI-VOCA for volunteers who are experts in farm management in animal husbandry.

4) Renew efforts to increase the milk yields. They are about one half of American yields. There are many companies like Monsanto where they can provide advice on feed programs and rations for cows. This will enhance your profitability.

5) More up-to-date sanitation procedures should be put in place. Much of the equipment had milk stone deposits due to lack of good cleaning chemicals. Companies selling cleaning supplies can set up a program for the actual daily procedures required to keep equipment clean.

6) Contact food seasoning companies about samples of flavoring that can be added to gouda cheese and chip dip products. The manufacture of food ingredients is a science in itself. They can be beneficially helpful with the innovation of new product development.

7) The standard plate count of the raw milk was over 500,000 which is border line for making quality cheese. It should be less than 50,000. Take line samples from the time the cows are milked to the refrigerated milk tanks and when it arrives in the cheese plant to determine the source of contamination.

8) Post-contamination: My tests indicated that coliform and E. coli was numerous in the finished product. E coli can cause serious outbreaks of intestinal illnesses which can cause loss of creditability in your business. This has happened in the US and can destroy your reputation and creditability quickly. I had observed people working in the plant that were not properly trained in the proper sanitation techniques. This affects the shelf life of the cheese and its quality. Lengthen curing time at proper temperatures to produce maximum flavor and texture.

Summary

Senaki Dairy is a unique company, a combined milk dairy farm and cheese production facility. It is a first class operation with many dedicated employees. Because of all the political strife and confrontation much of its industry and economics have been virtually destroyed. Much of the dairy products produced are only sold in nearby open markets. This plant has a viable opportunity to expand its operations as Georgian economy rebounds.

I discussed how we have been in the cheese business for over 55 years starting with a very small family operation and now sell out cheese products in every state in the US. I feel that this cheese operation could parallel ours in your country.

This is part of my final report to ACDI-VOCA. My final days in Georgia were devoted to touring interesting sites in the country.

Georgia is a fascinating country. I have to thank Gocha Mchedlisili, my driver, and my project director Nino Chanturia for taking time to show me their country. I remember just before I left for Georgia a package arrived at my house in the US. It contained a laptop computer with these instructions. Would I carry this in my luggage and give it to Nino Chanturia. I felt a little ill at ease carrying a valuable computer from a stranger and present it to someone I have never met. When I first met Nino and gave her the laptop computer she hugged it like it was her baby. Laptop computers were very popular and sought after. Nino was a great help traveling with me to the cheese plant and helping me make cheese. She was a friend of the owner of the cheese plant, Kakhar Alania. We would often go over to his house for dinner.

We drove several hundred kilometers to the shores of the Black Sea at Poti. They had friends who owned a restaurant and disco where we had a few beers and something to eat. A friend had a summer home near the shores of the Black Sea. I was invited to return with my wife and have use of his summer home. At the time I was already planning my next trip to Georgia accompanied by my wife, Trudy. On the return trip we stopped at some ruins along the old Silk Road where caravans changed camels and stayed overnight.

Historic Silk Road

The Silk Road is the transportation route which began in China and made its way through Central Asia and into Europe.

China was the earliest country to raise silk worms and produce silk garments. This was kept secret for over 1000 years. People in the eastern part of the world had no idea how this fabric was made. Many people thought it was actually an agricultural plant or a tree that was the source silk, nobody understood that it was produced by a worm.

These countries and regions also turned into diplomatic missions to China. It was a busy trade route, not only for silk but other products from Asia that were introduced in Europe. There are many books and journals about the Silk Road going back thousands of years. Marco Polo came to Beijing along the Silk Road in 1275 and gave detailed descriptions in his journals about local customs and cultures along the routes they traveled.

Along the Silk Road there are many ruins, passes, castles, grottoes, caves and fortresses where caravans would seek safety at night. We were able to visit a few of these sites. How they could travel such long distances and survive on these expeditions.

On our return to Tbilisi I noticed a sign, exit to the city of Gori, but nothing about Stalin. I thought it would be of great interest to visit his birthplace. I ask Gocha if we could visit the city. He seemed disinterested and indifferent about his country's relationship with Russia. He said there is only a small museum and the house where he was born, and it was not worth the time it would take to go there and time was running short. This was quite contrary to what I had read about Gori. The name of Stalin is notorious and synonymous with fear and terror.

No human being has ever destroyed so many millions of people and put them to their deaths in gulags and executions. I still notice in Russia that Stalinists still hail him as a hero. They say the country could not have defeated Germany or become a superpower without his leadership.

There is an old castle in Gori that has been rebuilt that dates back to the first century. There is also the Stalin Museum, enshrined within it is a pavilion with a small wooden hut were Stalin was born. Included in the museum are many of his personal items and journals.

I was in high school at the time of the Yalta Conference and we had a current events class instead of a history class. We would get a newspaper specially printed for students in high school with all the events relating to the war and post-war Europe. I found this quite interesting because my father and mother were born in Germany and were concerned about their families. I can remember my father hated Stalin and was so happy that his family resided in West Germany instead of the Russian zone of East Germany or Berlin. I hope sometime in the future when I return to Georgia I will make another effort to travel to the city of Gori.

I returned to Tbilisi and attended a wedding of a friend of Kakhar Alania. These weddings last for several days and they invite hundreds of people, even everyone from the nearby village. There was a huge banquet hall filled with so much food and alcohol and they stared to celebrate long before the bride and groom arrived. When I arrived everyone had quite a bit to drink already. They knew I wasn't a native Georgian so they introduced me as, Terrorist Osama Bin Laden's brother. My friend said he has 54 siblings and they wouldn't question it because everyone is welcome at a Georgian wedding. Everyone laughed and I told them I was just a token America cheese maker. Of course that called for another round of drinks and a toast. These are precious moments I will cherish for a long time. The following morning I was debriefed at ACDI-VOCA office and I spent the day writing up my final report. They wanted to know when I could make arrangements to return and teach them how to make processed cheese.

IT IS VERY COLD HERE IN OUR ROOM

My Russian translator Nina and I are huddled in our room trying to keep warm. We were given bags of shelled corn stalks to burn. They burn very quickly and the heat is short lived. We just bundled up and made the best of it and made a lot of hot tea on our stove.

There was a certain adventure to experience what the ordinary Georgian people had to endure daily.

There was a gas crisis in the Ukraine and Georgia. Gasprom, Russia's largest gas monopoly cut off gas supplies because of lingering disputes about payment and pricing. Moscow was facing severe economic problems because of fall of gas prices. The Ukraine and Georgia balked at the payment of these new higher prices. Then Turkmenistan turned off the gas shipments to Georgia. There has always been a politically motivated confrontation between Russia, Georgia and Ukraine because they wanted to join up with NATO threatening Russia sphere of influence in the area. Another provoking issue was the conflict between North and South Ossetia part of Georgia. This was partially politically motivated to punish the Georgian people. They also boycotted Georgian wine and Georgian produce

Return to Altai Republic – **Kirova Farm**

I received a call from the Washington DC office of ACDI-VOCA requesting my return to this part of Russia. I completed an assignment 2003 in the Altai and began reminiscing how beautiful this part of Russia was. I immediately accepted the assignment and signed a contract to complete this project receiving this information concerning my scope of work and proposed scheduling.

HOST:
Name: *"Kirova" Farm*
Primary: Adrey Yakovlevich Gagelgans, Director
Address   Podsosnova village, Nemetsky Natsionalny Okrug, Altai
Krai

I met my interpreter, Tatiana Tarabrina a very talented school teacher who spoke English and German. She was divorced and had a seven-year-old daughter. She had received a release time to travel with me to Podsosnova village, (it literally means under the pine tree). We did travel at least 5 hours by car over miles of gravel roads. We did encounter its first snow fall. It was a fascinating place. They had their own farm and milk processing plant. It literally was a Russian German village where most of the people that I worked with could speak German. They even had their own brewery which was very small and supplied the village with beer. Every evening we bought some beer and drank it with our supper that we would make by ourselves. This brew would only last for a day and then it would go flat but it was refreshing when consumed right after it was brewed. It must be part of the German tradition.

I wanted to mainly focus on broadening their product lines with new types of cheese and improve their quality and maybe try to reduce the cost of production of this plant.

FARMER-TO-FARMER CONSORTIUM
"OM" Limited Liability Company
DAIRY PRODUCTS TECHNOLOGY IMPROVEMENT

B. Project Location: Country: Russia Oblast/Krai: Stavropol
D. Summary of Assignment:

The FtF Consortium will require a technologist to assist the "OM" dairy plant in improving the quality of current products and developing new milk powder-based products. The volunteer will also assist with the quality analysis of the current butter and sour cream produced by the company and identify ways to improve it; the volunteer is also expected to provide recommendations on dairy products shelf life extension.

REQUESTING ORGANIZATION
Name: "OM" Limited Liability Company
Primary Contact: Oleg Ivanovich Egorov, Director

The steady up trend of consumption growth is an objective

Long-term

The long-term plans of the "OM" Dairy Plant company include increasing the volume of dairy products produced, thus increasing the sales revenue and company's profitability.

The volunteer is asked to advice on what by-products in addition to sour cream and butter can be produced on the company's equipment. The company would like to obtain recommendations on possibility of producing the so-called mix products, such as processed cheese or cream cheese spread and drinks based on milk/fermented milk with the addition of fruit juices.

I flew back to Moscow, had a debriefing at ADCI-VOCA office and departed for the US.

FARMER-TO-FARMER CONSORTIUM
"Sosnovsky" Cheese Plant
CHEESE PRODUCTION
B. Project Location: Country: Russia Oblast/Krai: Omsk oblast
         January 12, 2004 D. Summary of Assignment:
The FtF Consortium will field a specialist skilled in milk processing and cheese production to assist the "Sosnovsky" Cheese plant with advanced methods of hard and soft cheese production. In his work with the company the volunteer will also focus on quality improvement and cost effects of processed cheese currently produced at Sosnovsky as well as on development of new types of cheeses.

A. Name: Sosnovsky Cheese Plant, Limited Liability
Company
Primary Contact: Vadim Borisovich Tribushinin, Director
Address: Omsk oblast, Azovsky Nemetski Natsionalny
Raion, Sosnovka

C. Assignment Background

The "Sosnovsky" Cheese Plant is a brand new enterprise built "from scratch" in the spring of 2003. Vadim Tribushinin and two of his partners acquired a two-story brick building in the village of Sosnovka., and decided to organize a dairy processing operation there. The partners purchased simple small-capacity equipment and started making processed cheese. Sosnovsky purchases skim milk, hard cheese, low-fat cheese, milk margarine and flavorings as raw materials and processes them into so-called "sausage-cheese" (the processed cheese packed in a casing that looks like sausage). The company doesn't currently use any soybean-based additives and doesn't use a smoker trying to distinguish itself from other processed cheese producers as a high-quality natural or organic product. The company is going to purchase a batching pressure-gun for manufacturing small nylon-plastic packaged items (flavored processed cheese or other).

There are two medium-scale dairies located nearby that Sosnovsky has procurement contracts with. The Sosnovsky management has a plan to buy partial ownership of one of these dairy operations (currently unprofitable and poorly managed) in order to be less dependent on milk prices.

III. Description of Volunteer Assignment Problem Statement:

The Sosnovsky Company has a progressive management team eager to offer new products to the local market. The company already succeeded in introducing a high-quality processed cheese product to the Omsk oblast market: the Sosnovsky "sausage-cheese". The potential of the operation, however, is limited now by a lack of professional expertise needed to continuously upgrade the technology and introduce new products thus keeping up with market demands.

The management of the enterprise wants to adopt up-to-date cost efficient technologies of cheese production in order to improve their current business and would like to invite an FtF volunteer to help improve the cheese processing operation.

Return to Omsk

Sept 26, 2004 Sunday

I left from Buffalo, arrived at JFK and boarded Delta flight 31 for Moscow. When I arrived on Monday my driver picked me up and took me to the Varshava Hotel. The following day I was briefed and boarded Siberian Airlines to Omsk Siberia.

I was picked up by Alexey Darydon and taken to the hotel. The next day we went to the office for a final briefing. Olesya Maksimova came over with her father and took me to the cheese plant.

A friend of Vadim, Vladimir Lisemkov and his partner Valinto, had a plant 200 kilometers away. We went there to demonstrate some of our cheese products. Several women from his office sat in on my demonstration. He also brought about five different cheeses from five different cheese plants in the nearby area to evaluate. They were all very similar, just labeled Russian cheese. They tasted all alike to me. I tried to answer all his questions. Although he showed great interest he felt a bit pessimistic about the future of Russia. It also turned out they were looking for investors. I had enough experience in Russia to know if a project had potential. He wanted to build a new cheese plant but it was not very promising.

Upon completing this project Olesya and I toured the city visiting an art and a history museum where there were wax figures of famous Russians. That evening we went to a restaurant and had a dinner and attended an American Jazz concert. I returned to my hotel and wrote up my final report for the Washington before my departure to the US.

Accomplishment

I had brief meeting with Eric Shoger, an American who owns 12 pizza parlors and a restaurant in Novosibirsk. He would like to purchase Italian style mozzarella like we produce in the US. There is a possibility we could produce this here in Russia in this start-up plant. I will send all the necessary information to Slava. He will have it translated for them.

I traveled to Omsk on a night train where met with my translator Olesya Maksimova and Vadim Tribushinin. He and other investors are constructing a new cheese facility in the village of Sosnovka. They presently produce approximately 6 metric tons of processed cheese at another location. Their aim is to complete construction of a new facility in Sosnovka, take in raw milk and also make natural cheese.

Next I demonstrated at the agricultural University in Omsk how to make cheddar cheese curds. We purchased some raw milk on the open market. Vadim recorded all the procedures, moisture and PH requirements. The cheese turned out well and I also had many different spices herbs and flavorings which we added to the product.

331773 "Kaloriya" Closed Joint Stock Company
BRIE CHEESE TECHNOLOGY IMPROVEMENT
Travel dates: September 17 - September 29,
Scope of Work
"Kaloriya" Company

BRIE CHEESE TECHNOLOGY IMPROVEMENT

I. PROJECT INFORMATION

B. Project Location: Country: RussiaOblast/Krai: Krasnodar
April 25

The FtF Consortium will require a food technologist to assist the "Kaloriya" company in brie cheese production technology improvement. The volunteer will help with analysis of current brie cheese and identify ways to improve it.

Contact Information:

10 Rosanova Ulitsa, Biding 1 Moscow, Russia
Mr. Stanislav Kokosyan, Regional Program Manager
Ms. Karina Klimova, Project Manager
Ms. Irina Tkacheva, Project Manager
ACDI/VOCA - Stavropol

In 2006 Kaloriya started brie cheese production with white mold. They use MM-100 cultures of the "Danisko" company. The mold appears on the 5th-7th days. Humidity and temperature are the same, but mold doesn't grow uniformly. Cheese should be soft and of appropriate texture in 15 days. The company achieves the required results only in 30 days. Brie cheese is packaged in foil. When it is unpackaged it has ammonium flavor and a lot of white mold remains on the foil.

Camembert and Brie Production in Russia

I received a request to go to Russia to assist "Kaloriya" Cheese Plant in camembert and brie cheese technology. These types of cheeses are finding a market in a number of upscale markets in Moscow and other large Russian cities. I made camembert cheese when I was at the University of Wisconsin, but have not made it in many years. This was always one of my favorite cheeses so I decided to start producing this cheese on a laboratory scale in our US plant. I worked on it for about thirty days making dozens of different methods that I could take to Russia with me. It is a unique cheese of a mold variety which has a snow white mold on the surface.

I flew to Moscow and was briefed at ACDI-VOCA office and boarded a flight to Krasnodar. I was met at the airport by Nataliya Kopeikina, my interpreter. We traveled about one hour by car to the hotel Stanitsa Kanevskaya. The following morning we went to the plant and began working. I detailed all my work in my final report. It was one of my most interesting assignments and felt privileged to be involved in this project. It was also a learning experience for me.

On my return to Moscow I took some of my brie that I had made and presented it to the office staff at ACDI-VOCA. They always looked forward to different cheeses that we had made. They would buy some wine and we would have a wine and cheese tasting. They were so surprised that we could make this type of cheese in Russia. This is now the only plant in Russia making camembert and brie cheese. Before, it had to be imported from France. Yelena Savinova, my Deputy Project Director said, "we are surely making progress in our cheese industry in Russia". There is no reason why we can't make world quality cheese products in Russia.

On the last few days we made some American style cottage

cheese. We had several failures due to improper acid development. This is very critical to obtain the proper curd formations. After a failure it become very stressful because you have come so far and they are expecting great results and are anxious to learn all this new technology. They always said to me we know enough about cheese making to realize that it takes time to develop a new product. We will have some more milk ready in the morning and we will try again. There is no better feeling when everything turns out well.

Everywhere I went in Russia they produce a cottage cheese like our farmers cheese which was called tvorog. It is very acidy. We add a sweet cream dressing that raises the pH and sweetens it for a delicious cheese to add to a salad.

MOLD RIPENED CHEESE
Basic steps in domestic Camembert manufacture.
Top left: Adding starter,
Top right: Cutting curd.
Bottom left: dipping.
Bottom right: Turning forms.

Camembert Cheese - American Style

Setting the Milk
8:00 A.M.

Pasteurize fresh, whole milk at 161.6°F (72°C) for 16 sec., and cool it to 90°F (32.2°C). Pump the milk directly into a standard cheese vat. Stir 2.0% active lactic starter into the warm, incoming milk. Acid-ripen the milk, for 15-30 min. Addition of color is optional; use up to 7 ml. annatto color per 1,000 lb. milk, Figure 182.

When the titratable acidity of the milk is 0.22 percent, introduce single-strength (1:15,000) rennet extract, 3-1/2 oz. (100 'ml.), per 1,000 lb. milk. Rennet extract is diluted 1:40 with tap water. Mix well for 3 min., cover the vat, and leave the milk quiescent. A very strong curd is desired, so the setting time is 45 min.

Cutting the Curd
9:30 A.M.

When the curd is properly firmed cut it into cubes with 5/8-in. knives. The curd alternatively can be dipped, Figure 182.

Cooking the Curds
9:45 A.M.
No change in cooking at elevated temperatures is required. Maintain the 90°F (32.2°C) temperature.

Dipping of Curds
9:45 A.M.
Ladle the intact curd, or, within 15 minutes after cutting, both the curds and whey, into open-ended, perforated, 8-oz. stainless steel, round molds. These metal forms rest on bamboo or nylon drainage mats which are on draining tables. Carefully fill the forms to capacity once. Let them drain and do not add any more curds to the molds, Figure 182.

Draining the Whey
10:30 A.M.

Apply no external pressure to the curds in the molds. In several hours, at room temperature about 72°F (22.2°C), the curds have been drained enough to be turned without breaking. After about three hours of drainage, turn the mold for the first time with a quick flip. Turning is facilitated by placing a flat metal plate on top before flipping. Repeat the turning of the cheese after another two hours. Turn 3-4 times more at 30-min. intervals, Figure 182.

Inoculating P. camemberti Spores
4:30 P.M.
　　With a spray gun, disseminate a fine mist of P. camemberti var. Thom aqueous spore suspension over the curd wheels, Figure 61, making one pass over the cheese surfaces. In 30 min., turn the cheese molds and repeat the single application spore suspension spraying. This is the extent of inoculation. Leave the cheese rest in their molds for 30 min. after the second spraying.

Pressing and Molding the Curd
5:30 P.M.
　　Remove the small wheels of curd from their molds with a spatula. Place them on clean drainage mats and leave exposed on the table in a clean room at about 72°F (22.2°C) for 5-6 hr. Usually no weights are placed on the surface.

Salting the Curd
11:00 P. M.
　　Pick up a wheel of the curd and dip one-half of it into a pail of coarse salt, Figure [55]. Shake off any loose salt, reverse the cheese, and dip the unsalted side in the pail in the same manner. Lay the salted cheese on draining boards and leave it, with all the others, overnight at room temperature. A mechanical or electronic salting device may be used instead.

Curing
One Day Later-8:00 A.M.
　　Transfer the cheeses to a 50°F (10°C) and 95-98% relative humidity room. Place them on cane racks, slightly elevated from the curing shelves. The cheese remains in this position, undisturbed, for 5 days. As soon as white whiskers of mold appear on the surface, turn over the wheel once. After 14 days in the curing room, Figure 183, wrap the wheels in tinfoil and store at 50°F (10°C) and 95% relative humidity for 7 days. Then move them to a cold room, 40°F (4.4°C), in the same condition. Cut the wheels into consumer wedges, if required.
Re-wrapping and distribution follow immediately.

Distribution
Camembert cheese cannot be stored for any length of time, as ripening continues even at low temperatures. Start moving the chilled cheese to distribution channels as soon as possible after the final packaging. It should be in the hands of wholesalers within one week after final packaging and in the hands of the consumer within two to three weeks.

Summary

I have traveled across Russia making 30 trips in the past 12 years. There have been many changes in the Russian dairy industry. Their economy is growing at 8% a year. In the private sector, farmers are lagging behind, especially milk producers. There are still milk deficits during the winter months. Milk yields are low compared to European and American counterparts.

Processing plants have greatly improved as evidenced by the Kaloriya plant. The Agricultural Minister in Russia needs to step forward and set sanitary regulations. The rules and regulations need to be strictly enforced to assure only high quality milk is allowed to enter processing plants. When you conduct dairy seminars, it would be a great topic to discuss. There is a tremendous amount of new technology and information from our US Agricultural Universities available to everyone on animal husbandry and feed production for dairy cows to increase yields in milk production. Dairy farming needs to be profitable to sustain itself.

My utmost admiration goes to the General Director, Natalya Dmitrievna Boeva, Olga Vladimirova Shabanova, Chief Technologist, Marina Vladimirova Fedorenko and their staff for what they have accomplished after Perestroika. They are a very progressive organization. The Kaloriya Company will become a leader and innovator in Russia's future.

I would like to thank ACDI-VOCA, the host organization and especially Natatya Kopeikina who helped with all my translations for my assignment. If there is any further information I could provide in the future, I would be happy to assist.

Yelena thanked me for all the work projects I have completed in my 12 years working in Russia. This was my last assignment. Volunteering for ACDI-VOCA gave me an opportunity few Americans had to travel to so many parts of Russia, learn to speak the language and meet and work with so many friendly and interesting people. ACDI-VOCA closed their offices in Russia but would continue working in other parts of the world.

My View of Russia Several Years After My Work Was Completed

On December 31, 1999 Boris Yeltsin made a stunning announcement of his leaving office. He said he wanted his country to enter into a new leadership in the new millennium. He had chosen a successor, Prime Minister Vladimir Putin. Yeltsin was extremely unpopular. It was estimated his approval ratings were 2%. Most political analysts stated he did this to save his own skin. Eventually he could have been arrested as so many former Soviet leaders that were ousted.

He struggled with alcoholism and neurological disorders and died on April 23, 2007. He was buried in the Novodevichy Cemetery. I often visited the cemetery while in Moscow. Many notable Soviets lie in this cemetery. He also was the first Soviet leader to die in peaceful retirement having overseen a peaceful transfer to his successor.

Vladimir Putin became president in December 31, 1999 when Boris Yeltsin resigned in a surprise move. Many political commentators said he eventually could have been impeached for destroying his own country. Putin allowed him to retire into oblivion. Putin won the 2000 election and in 2004 was reelected for a second term. In 2008 Dmitry Medvedev became president and he nominated Vladimir Putin Prime Minister. It always seemed to me that Putin was much more visible in the media than Medvedev.

Putin's achievements have been described as a result of a tenfold increase in oil prices. Most Russians felt Boris Yeltsin was responsible for the disastrous privatization of all the state owned assets. He will always be remembered for allowing the Kremlin insiders to steal or seize assets at fire-sale prices. Since the turn-of-the-century many Russians are becoming more affluent and also demanding more consumer goods. Many young people are flocking to the cities and entering universities in search of opportunity and higher paying jobs.

Putin has overseen a return to political stability and economic progress in Russia from the severe crisis of the 1990s. During his presidency the Russian economy grew for nine straight years

Most Russians I have become acquainted with enjoy our friendship. They have told me you Americans have developed the World Wide Web. This gives us an opportunity to access all major newspapers and publications on our computers. Your democracy may fit your way of life. Many Russians admire the socialistic countries like Norway, Sweden and Denmark. We will hopefully tailor our life and democracy to fit our needs. I feel that the populations of all democratic countries, including Russia, with today's youth will witness a less confrontational and be more unwarlike society in their generation. Hopefully this is one of my dreams to come true.

A Lasting Memory: Vladimir Lenin's Body in His Mausoleum in Red Square

On one of my last trips to Moscow there was an article in the Moscow Times. If you wish to view Vladimir Lenin's body it may be your last chance before his removal for burial. I called Lyudmila, an elderly lady whom I had met. She was an interrupter. I would call upon her as a guide when I visited museums or historic places in Moscow. She knew her history but she always had her own opinion on how it really was.

She thought the article in the Moscow Times was a way of marketing a product that was losing its appeal. I had noticed there were no more lines in front of the mausoleum. I thought it was closed. She said I will meet you in Red square. I can always remember pictures in our American newspapers, long lines of Russians standing for hours to catch a glimpse of Vladimir Lenin lying in his tomb since his death in 1924. Lyudmila said the news media always brings up the fact that they are going to bury him. This was just to generate some interest to get people to view his body.

This is how things have changed in Russia. When Lenin's burial was proposed, Vladimir Putin proposed a referendum. 70% of the people voted for Lenin's removal and burial. It was an era gone by and they should move on. He is part of our history and he will be remembered for his accomplishments good and bad.

Gennadi Zyuanov, head of the Communist Party went understandably ballistic, any talk about a burial is ludicrous and vulgar and to rewrite our history is unspeakable. So many Russians who sacrificed their lives in World War II could never comprehend why any Russian could even contemplate in his mind to erase the memory of Vladimir Lenin.

My wife Trudy and I traveled together on this trip to Moscow and met Lyudmila. Just a few people arrived as the mausoleum opened and we immediately entered. There were military guards who took our cameras and returned them as we exited. They were very stern informing us no picture taking and you had to be silent and move through in an orderly manner, showing respect.

There were thousands of people in Red square on this beautiful cold Sunday morning. I thought to myself in Soviet times in the cold of the winter they would stand in line for hours waiting just to pay their respects and grab a quick glance of Vladimir Lenin. Why not anymore? I got a perception that Lyudmila felt a little mournful when she saw some older Russian peasants carrying signs in Support of Joseph Stalin.

I thought to myself what if in America George Washington was embalmed and lying in state at Mount Vernon? I can imagine thousands of Americans would want to witness that.

Kutter's Cheese Factory/Yancey's Fancy: Bright Future
March 15, 2013

"Kutter's /Yancey's Fancy has experienced tremendous growth sales" said, Brian Bailey, Yancey's Fancy Vice President of Operations.   Presently, the company offers 45 varieties of cheese nationwide and they are also sold at the Kutter's cheese factory store located at the manufacturing facility.

During my semi-retirement years, and while not in Russia, I was heavily involved in research and development of new cheese products. We were one of the first cheese plants to introduce high intensity flavored cheeses such as horseradish, garlic, onion champagne and an assortment of hot and sweet pepper varieties.

171

Kutters/Yancey's Fancy won first place in a world cheese contest with entries from countries around the world. We were sponsored by Wisconsin Cheese Makers Association for our Jalapeno Peppadew cheese and also received many awards at the New York State Fair.

Kutter's Cheese Factory/Yancey's Fancy Expansion

Genesee County Economic Development Corp: Reported on a proposed expansion plan to triple size of Yancey's Fancy manufacturing facility from 30,000 square feet to 102,000 square feet. Expect capital expenditure upwards of $20,000,000. To be completed by late 2014.

Once completed the work force should increase from 120 to 175 employees. "We've outgrown our plant. We can't meet out production requirements to fill our orders from increased deals with national retailers and super market chains" said Brian Bailey. Yancey's Fancy will a retain 40,000 square foot cold storage facility in Batavia. The company now produces 9 million lbs. of cheese yearly.

Constructing the addition of a new $20,000,000 plant for process cheese manufacturing allowing tripling of production. Estimated date of completion: November 2014

The plant generates over a million lbs. of whey weekly which has been used for animal feed at a great loss. It will be installing new membrane technology to concentrate whey for foods used in multitudes of nutritional human foods. New modern cheese making equipment and packaging lines will be increased.

66 years ago when Leo Kutter and his two sons started the business it was a father and son operation. Leo Kutter passed away at 69 and sons Richard and Tony continued until John Yancey and later Dietz and Watson took over.

My father would be so proud to see what his cheese company has accomplished.

If there was one more accomplishment I could achieve it would be to build a cheese museum. I have saved so much of the old cheese making equipment and acquired some more for this project. In 1924, when my father began to run a small cheese factory for Hassellbeck Cheese Company, electricity was non-existent in rural areas, it was all steam powered. It would make a great museum along with a visitor's center.

Demonstrating how cheese was made on an open fire by Leo Kutter
at the turn of the century in the Bavarian Alps.

Nico Van Zwanenberg: former owner of Cuba Cheese and
Trading Company, a very good friend of mine, demonstrating
how cheese is made.

Come and visit us!

Pictures

Myself, and my co-workers at Senaki cheese plant in Georgia.

Turning over Neudochino cheese plant to the village.

Vania, Tony, Tonya

Main Street Neudochino village: picking up milk for cheese
plant

House and vegetable garden where I lived

St Petersburg cheese plant: Maria, Tony, and Pat Tatyana

St Petersburg cheese plant: Maria, Tony, Livinova,
Tatyana

Children going to school in Neudochino Siberia,
temperature 5 degrees below zero

School children are daring the boy to throw
a snowball at me

Caucasus Mountains

More Sheep on the Road

The following is from CIA Factbook.

(www.cia.gov/library/publications/the-world-factbook/geos/xx.html)

Introduction Russia

Background: Founded in the 12th century, the Principality of Muscovy was able to emerge from over 200 years of Mongol domination (13th-15th centuries) and to gradually conquer and absorb surrounding principalities. In the early 17th century, a new Romanov Dynasty continued this policy of expansion across Siberia to the Pacific. Under PETER I (ruled 1682-1725), hegemony was extended to the Baltic Sea and the country was renamed the Russian Empire. During the 19th century, more territorial acquisitions were made in Europe and Asia. Repeated devastating defeats of the Russian army in World War I led to widespread rioting in the major cities of the Russian Empire and to the overthrow in 1917 of the imperial household. The Communists under Vladimir LENIN seized power soon after and formed the USSR. The brutal rule of Josef STALIN (1928-53) strengthened Russian dominance of the Soviet Union at a cost of tens of millions of lives. The Soviet economy and society stagnated in the following decades until General Secretary Mikhail GORBACHEV

(1985-91) introduced glasnost (openness) and perestroika (restructuring) in an attempt to modernize Communism, but his initiatives inadvertently released forces that by December 1991 splintered the USSR into 15 independent republics. Since then, Russia has struggled in its efforts to build a democratic political system and market economy to replace the strict social, political, and economic controls of the Communist period. While some progress has been made on the economic front, recent years have seen a recentralization of power under Vladimir PUTIN and an erosion in nascent democratic institutions. A determined guerrilla conflict still plagues Russia in Chechnya.

Geography Russia

Location: Northern Asia (that part west of the Urals is included with Europe), bordering the Arctic Ocean, between Europe and the North Pacific Ocean

Geographic coordinates: 60 00 N, 100 00 E

Map references: Asia

Area: *total:* 17,075,200 sq km
water: 79,400 sq km
land: 16,995,800 sq km

Area - comparative: approximately 1.8 times the size of the US

Land boundaries: *total:* 20,017 km
border countries: Azerbaijan 284 km, Belarus 959 km, China (southeast) 3,605 km, China (south) 40 km, Estonia 294 km, Finland 1,340 km, Georgia 723 km, Kazakhstan 6,846 km, North Korea 19 km, Latvia 217 km, Lithuania (Kaliningrad Oblast) 227 km, Mongolia 3,485 km, Norway 196 km, Poland (Kaliningrad Oblast) 206 km, Ukraine 1,576 km

Coastline:	37,653 km
Maritime claims:	*territorial sea:* 12 nm *exclusive economic zone:* 200 nm *continental shelf:* 200-m depth or to the depth of exploitation
Climate:	ranges from steppes in the south through humid continental in much of European Russia; subarctic in Siberia to tundra climate in the polar north; winters vary from cool along Black Sea coast to frigid in Siberia; summers vary from warm in the steppes to cool along Arctic coast
Terrain:	broad plain with low hills west of Urals; vast coniferous forest and tundra in Siberia; uplands and mountains along southern border regions
Elevation extremes:	*lowest point:* Caspian Sea -28 m *highest point:* Gora El'brus 5,633 m
Natural resources:	wide natural resource base including major deposits of oil, natural gas, coal, and many strategic minerals, timber *note:* formidable obstacles of climate, terrain, and distance hinder exploitation of natural resources
Land use:	*arable land:* 7.33% *permanent crops:* 0.11% *other:* 92.56% (2001)
Irrigated land:	46,630 sq km (1998 est.)
Natural hazards:	permafrost over much of Siberia is a major impediment to development; volcanic activity in the Kuril Islands; volcanoes and earthquakes on the Kamchatka Peninsula; spring floods and summer/autumn forest fires throughout Siberia and parts of European Russia
Environment - current issues:	air pollution from heavy industry, emissions of coal-fired electric plants, and transportation in major cities; industrial, municipal, and agricultural pollution of inland waterways and seacoasts; deforestation; soil erosion; soil contamination from improper application of

agricultural chemicals; scattered areas of sometimes intense radioactive contamination; groundwater contamination from toxic waste; urban solid waste management; abandoned stocks of obsolete pesticides

Environment - international agreements: *party to:* Air Pollution, Air Pollution-Nitrogen Oxides, Air Pollution-Sulfur 85, Antarctic-Environmental Protocol, Antarctic-Marine Living Resources, Antarctic Seals, Antarctic Treaty, Biodiversity, Climate Change, Endangered Species, Environmental Modification, Hazardous Wastes, Law of the Sea, Marine Dumping, Ozone Layer Protection, Ship Pollution, Tropical Timber 83, Wetlands, Whaling
signed, but not ratified: Air Pollution-Sulfur 94, Climate Change-Kyoto Protocol

Geography - note: largest country in the world in terms of area but unfavorably located in relation to major sea lanes of the world; despite its size, much of the country lacks proper soils and climates (either too cold or too dry) for agriculture; Mount El'brus is Europe's tallest peak

People	Russia

Population: 143,782,338 (July 2004 est.)

Age structure: *0-14 years:* 15% (male 11,064,109; female 10,518,595)
15-64 years: 71.3% (male 49,534,076; female 52,958,107)
65 years and over: 13.7% (male 6,177,580; female 13,529,871) (2004 est.)

Median age: *total:* 37.9 years
male: 34.7 years
female: 40.7 years (2004 est.)

Population growth rate: -0.45% (2004 est.)

Birth rate: 9.63 births/1,000 population (2004 est.)

Death rate: 15.17 deaths/1,000 population (2004 est.)

Net migration rate: 1.02 migrant(s)/1,000 population (2004 est.)

Made in the USA
Charleston, SC
14 October 2014